KEYS *to* FOLLOWING JESUS

Learn How Jesus Acted, And Reacted To Situations <u>He Faced When He Walked This Earth.</u>

Jan Wilson

Copyright © 2014 by Jan Wilson

Keys To Following Jesus
Learn How Jesus Acted, And Reacted To Situations He Faced When He Walked This Earth.
by Jan Wilson

Printed in the United States of America

ISBN 9781629527000

All rights reserved solely by the author. The author guarantees all contents are original and do not infringe upon the legal rights of any other person or work. No part of this book may be reproduced in any form without the permission of the author. The views expressed in this book are not necessarily those of the publisher.

Unless otherwise indicated, Scripture is taken from the King James Version of the Bible, *Public Domain.*

Scripture marked ESV is taken from The Holy Bible, English Starndard Version, copyright © 2001 by Crossway Bibles, a division of Good News Publishers. Used by permission. All rights reserved.

Scripture marked NIV is taken from the HOLY BIBLE, NEW INTERNATIONAL VERSION®. NIV®. Copyright © 1973, 1978, 1984 by International Bible Society. Used by permission of Zondervan. All rights reserved.

www.xulonpress.com

Keys represent knowledge. Keys lock and unlock and give us access to places. When Jesus said to Peter, "I will give unto thee the keys of the kingdom of heaven," He was saying, "I will give you access to the kingdom of heaven, to exercise dominion and power over demons and evil spirits (Matthew 16:19).

Know this; it's knowledge that will get you where you truly want to be! It's the knowledge of God's Word that will catapult or propel you from the level you are now to a higher level in life.

A hypocrite with his mouth destroyeth his neighbor: but through knowledge shall the just be delivered.
Proverbs 11:9

TABLE OF CONTENTS

Introduction ix

1. Our Position With Jesus Christ 11
2. Your Willingness To Follow 20
3. What Does It Means To Follow and Serve? 30
4. The Difference between David and Saul 45
5. Always Think Before Acting 67
6. Submit Yourself to God 83

Introduction

Many Christians haven't understood the difference between being a Christian and becoming a **FOLLOWER OF JESUS**. Being a Christian sets you apart unto God by the new birth that takes place in your spirit when you accept Jesus Christ into your heart. But that's not enough. You must renew your mind and have the **ATTITUDE OF JESUS**, and become a follower of Jesus! The Bible says,

...And be not conformed to this world: but be ye transformed by the renewing of your mind that ye may prove what is that good, and acceptable, and perfect will of God.
Romans 12:2

As you renew your mind through God's words, I can guarantee you will start to develop the attitude of Jesus. In this book I disclose scriptural keys, or principles, that will help you develop the attitude of Jesus as you fellow Him. Be sensitive to what the Spirit of God is saying to you as you read this book and study God's Word. Your life will never be the same when you obey these simple and power principles. God bless you!

CHAPTER 1

OUR POSITION WITH JESUS CHRIST

In order to be effective in your work with a company or organization, it's very important that you know your position in the organization. Your value to that company or organization will be limited without knowing your position, or where you stand with that company, or without knowing your reason for becoming a member of that organization.

These same rules apply to Christianity. In order to be effective in your walk with God, it is very important to know your position or assignment **with Jesus**. To know your position is to know your standing; you can't effectively carry out your assignment for Jesus without knowing your position.

Sadly, many of God's beloved children are not effective in their walk with Jesus today because their minds are closed to this truth found in God's Word. That's why we need these keys to unlock God's words in our minds and thus enlighten our spirit, soul, and body. Hallelujah! Praise God. Now, let's read what the Bible says about us.

Even when we were dead in sins, [he] hath quickened us together with Christ, (by grace ye are saved); And hath raised us up together, and made us sit together in heavenly places in Christ Jesus: That

in the ages to come He might shew the exceeding riches of his grace in his kindness toward us through Christ Jesus.
Ephesians 2:5-7

Paul here is writing to the church in Ephesus and to all Christians around the world. He's speaking under the influence of the Holy Spirit, telling us that we have been quickened by Jesus. We have been raised up together with Jesus Christ, and we are seated together in Jesus Christ, far above all principalities and powers.

The word *quickened* is a verb. It means to make more rapid, accelerate, or hasten, to give or restore vigor or activity to, stir up, rouse, or stimulate. Simply stated, it means to revive or restore life to a person or thing.

Listen, do you know your body is Jesus' body, and that Jesus' body is your body? Just ask yourself, where am I right now? I can guess you're probably in your room, at home, school, or some other place right here on this earth, reading this book. But if that is true, how can Jesus say you're seated together with Him in heavenly places? That is a revelation!

The Word of God is right: we're seated together with Christ in heaven, but it's in the spirit and not the physical. I told you that Jesus' body is our body and our body is Jesus' body; He is representing us in heaven, and we are representing Him here on earth. The Bible says,

Herein is our love made perfect, that we may have boldness in the Day of Judgment: <u>because as he is, so are we in this world</u>.
1 John 4:17

As Jesus is in heaven, so are we (His body) Christians in this world. We are like Him, acting like Him, living like Him, and walking like Him in this world. If this does not describe you, then this book is designed for you—to help you walk, act, and live as He did on this earth.

Sharers Together

Wherefore, holy brethren, <u>partakers</u> of the heavenly calling, consider the Apostle and High Priest of our profession, Christ Jesus.
Hebrews 3:1

The English Standard Version says that we're sharers together in the heavenly calling or heavenly life; Christ is the head of the body, the church.

We then, as <u>workers together with Him</u>, beseech you also that ye receive not the grace of God in vain.
2 Corinthians 6:1

And He is the head of the body, the church: who is the beginning, the firstborn from the dead; that in all things He might have the preeminence. For it pleased the Father that in Him should all fullness dwell.
Colossians 1:18-19

Beware lest any man spoil you through philosophy and vain deceit, after the tradition of men, after the rudiments of the world, and not after Christ. For in Him dwelleth all the fullness of the Godhead bodily. And ye are complete in Him, which is the head of all principality and power.
Colossians 2:8-10

Now listen; if all the fullness of God dwells in Jesus Christ, then all the fullness of God can be in us, because the Bible says that He is the true vine and we (the church) are the branches. It's just a matter of time. If you will continue your walk with Jesus, **the fullness of God will stand out big in you**. It's my prayer that you will grow and mature in the knowledge of God's Word. Amen!

Get Plugged-in to Jesus

I am the true vine and my Father is the husbandman. Every branch in me that beareth not fruit He taketh away: and every branch that beareth fruit, He purgeth it, that it may bring forth more fruit. Now ye are clean through the word which I have spoken unto you. Abide in me and I in you. As the branch cannot bear fruit of itself, except it abide in the vine; no more can ye, except ye abide in me.

I am the vine, ye are the branches: He that abideth in me, and I in him, the same bringeth forth much fruit: for without me ye can do nothing. If a man abides not in me, he is cast forth as a branch, and is withered; and men gather them, and cast them into the fire and they are burned.

If ye abide in me, and my words abide in you, ye shall ask what ye will, and it shall be done unto you. Herein is my Father glorified, that ye bear much fruit; so shall ye be my disciples. As the Father hath loved me, so have I loved you: continue ye in my love.

If ye keep my commandments, ye shall abide in my love; even as I have kept my Father's commandments, and abide in His love. These things have I spoken unto you, that my joy might remain in you, and that your joy might be full. <u>This is my commandment, that ye love one another, as I have loved you.</u>

Greater love hath no man than this that a man lay down his life for his friends. Ye are my friends, if ye do whatsoever I command you. Henceforth I call you not servants; for the servant knoweth not what his lord doeth: but I have called you friends; for all things that I have heard of my Father I have made known unto you.

Ye have not chosen me, but I have chosen you, and ordained you, that ye should go and bring forth fruit, and that your fruit should remain: that whatsoever ye shall ask of the Father <u>*in my name*</u>, *He may give it you. These things I command you, that ye love one another.*

John 15:1-17

Why is it so important for you to get plugged-in to Jesus? Because the Bible says by Him all things were created, both in heaven and on earth, and He is before all things, including your future! All things consist by Him, and He declares the end from the beginning.

For by Him were all things created, that are in heaven, and that are in earth, visible and invisible, whether they be thrones, or dominions, or principalities, or powers: all things were created by Him, and for him: And He is before all things, and by Him all things consist.
Colossians 1:16-17

...declaring the end from the beginning, and from ancient times the things that are not yet done, saying, My counsel shall stand, and I will do all my pleasure.
Isaiah 46:10

These are some of the reasons why you must get plugged-in, or connected, to Jesus. Remember, He said that without Him you can do nothing great in life. Your peace, strength, and success flow from Him. He is the vine, and we are the branches, and you know and I know that all branches live in the vine. **Without the vine, there is no life for the branches; without Jesus, there is no life for you!**

Jesus also said we must continue in His love in order to be true followers of Him. It is by continuing in His love that all men will know we are His followers. He said if we keep His commandments, this will enable us to abide in His love.

Let me tell you something you probably haven't heard before: **Love** is the only thing you will need to fellowship with God and to worship and praise God in heaven. If you can speak in tongues, you won't need that in heaven; if you can prophesy, you won't need that in heaven; if God has blessed you with the gift of healing and you're healing a lot of sick people here on this earth, you won't need that healing power in heaven, for there will be no sick people there to heal. Love is the only thing you will need to fellowship with God in heaven, because God is love and love is God!

And we have known and believed the love that God hath to us. <u>God is love; and he that dwelleth in love dwelleth in God and God in him</u>.
1 John 4:16

Let me tell you another revelation that you probably haven't heard before. Do you know that God said we should **love our neighbor as ourselves**? Yes, He did, and the main reason for this command is that we're the branches and He is the vine. If you take a look at a tree, you will notice that all the **branches are connected to the same trunk and thus to one another.** That's why He said, **"Love your neighbor as you love yourself"**— because **you are inside your neighbor**. Every one of us carries a **likeness of every other person, or an image of every other person, inside us**!

Jesus said unto him, Thou shalt love the Lord thy God with all thy heart, and with all thy soul, and with all thy mind. This is the first and great commandment. And the second is like unto it, Thou shalt love thy neighbor as thyself. <u>On these two commandments hang all the law and the prophets</u>.
Matthew 22:37-40

But so many people living today, including Christians, don't know this truth, because the god of this world (system), the devil, has blinded the minds of people, lest the light of the glorious gospel of Jesus Christ should shine on them and they see and believe the truth. But if you will continue with Jesus, then you will know and believe the truth, and the truth will set you free. Amen!

In whom the god of this world hath blinded the minds of them which believe not, lest the light of the glorious gospel of Christ, <u>who is the image of God</u>, should shine unto them.
2 Corinthians 4:4

Then said Jesus to those Jews which believed on him, if ye <u>continue in my word</u>, then are ye my disciples indeed; And ye shall <u>know the truth, and the truth shall make you free</u>.
John 8:31-32

Reasons Why We Gather

As a follower of Jesus Christ, one of those things that will enhance your fellowship with Him is gathering with other believers, or Christians. God didn't command us to have worship services for the sole purpose of hearing the pastor preach or singing worship songs and praises to Him.

These things are very good, of course, but they are not the primary reasons we are to gather together. The primary reason for going to worship services is for **strengthening the body** of Christ, or strengthening one another. It's for our own spiritual growth!

Let us hold fast the profession of our faith without wavering; (for he is faithful that promised); And let us <u>consider one another</u> to provoke unto <u>love</u> and to good works: <u>Not forsaking the assembling of ourselves together</u>, as the manner of some is; but <u>exhorting one another</u>: and so much the more, as ye see the day approaching.
Hebrews 10:23-25

Now, I want you to understand some very important words God is using here. I know He speaks about exhortation, and that's why I included preaching, because listening to God's Word being preached is very important for our spiritual growth. Indeed, **exhortation brings transformation, then transformation brings promotion, and promotion brings increase!** The Bible says we shouldn't be conformed to this world but transformed by renewing our minds through the Word of God; that's why exhortation is very important.

I beseech you therefore, brethren, by the mercies of God, that ye present your bodies a living sacrifice, holy, acceptable unto God, which is your reasonable service. And be not conformed to this world: but be ye transformed by the renewing of your mind, that ye may prove what is that good, and acceptable and perfect, will of God.
Romans 12:1-2

Another thing I want you to note here is that in the Hebrews passage God uses the words *one another* in both verse 24 and verse 25. You may ask why this is so important. It's important because that's the primary reason for our gathering; we gather for the purpose of **strengthening one another**, and God emphasized this by using these words twice.

Everybody that has a TV in the home has access to a gospel channel or can hear a pastor preach God's Word either on Sundays or weekdays. Back home in Africa, we were raised with having family devotions every morning and sometimes evening, so we got used to hearing God's Word everyday at home.

So you're not going to church on Sunday just to hear the pastor preach. You can hear that from home if you want. Most important, you go to church for the purpose of strengthening the body of Jesus Christ. Jesus wants His whole body to be strengthened, not just the head; this was in the mind of God when He was leading His servant to write this to all Christians scattered around the world.

Jesus said to Peter one day that Satan had desired to have him, but He prayed for Peter that his faith would not fail and that after his recovery he would strengthen his brethren:

And the lord said, Simon, Simon, behold, Satan hath desired to have you, that he may sift you as wheat: But I have prayed for thee, that thy faith fail not: and when thou art converted, <u>strengthen thy brethren</u>.
Luke 22:31-32

Jesus told Peter something strange when he wasn't even thinking that such a thing could happen to him. He said, "Simon, Satan has desired to have and sift you as wheat, but I have prayed for you." Jesus is still interceding for us, and He has commanded us to do the same for one another here on earth. To be an effective follower of Jesus, this should be our **number one job—prayer for one another**.

Confess your faults one to another, and <u>pray one for another</u>, that ye may be <u>healed</u>. The effectual fervent prayer of a righteous man availeth much.
James 5:16

Praying always with all prayer and supplication in the Spirit, and watching thereunto with all perseverance and supplication for <u>all saints</u>; And for me, that utterance may be given unto me, that I may open my mouth boldly, to make known the mystery of the gospel, For which I am an ambassador in bonds: That therein I may speak boldly, as I ought to speak.
Ephesians 6:18-20

My little children, these things write I unto you, that ye sin not. And if any man sin, we have an advocate with the Father, Jesus Christ the righteous.
1 John 2:1

Satan is still desiring and wishing to sift all Christians today. That's why we should always pray for each other. **Satan is against every follower of Jesus Christ**. The word *sift* means to **scatter or separate**. His desire is to scatter and separate God's people, but thanks be to God we're more than conquerors through Jesus Christ.

Nay, in all these things we are more than conquerors through Him that loved us.
Romans 8:37

CHAPTER 2

YOUR WILLINGNESS TO FOLLOW

...For the kingdom of heaven is like unto a man that is an householder, which went out early in the morning to hire labourers into his vineyard. And when he had agreed with the labourers for a penny a day, he sent them into his vineyard.

And he went out about the third hour, and saw others standing idle in the marketplace, and said unto them; Go ye also into the vineyard, and whatsoever is right I will give you. And they went their way.

Again he went out about the sixth and ninth hour, and did likewise. And about the eleventh hour he went out, and found others standing idle, and saith unto them, why stand ye here all the day idle? They say unto him, because no man hath hired us. He saith unto them, Go ye also into the vineyard; So when even was come, the lord of the vineyard saith unto his steward, Call the labourers, and give them their hire, beginning from the last unto the first. And when they came that were hired about the eleventh hour, they received every man a penny.

But when the first came, they supposed that they should have received more; and they likewise received every man a penny. And when they had received it, they murmured against the Goodman of the house, Saying, these last have wrought but one hour, and thou hast made them equal unto us, which have borne the burden and heat of the day.

But he answered one of them, and said, Friend, I do thee no wrong: didst not thou agree with me for a penny? Take that thine is, and go thy way: I will give unto this last, even as unto thee.

Is it not lawful for me to do what I will with mine own? Is thine eye evil, because I am good? So the last shall be first and the first last: for many be called, but few chosen.
Matthew 20:1-16

Your willingness to follow Jesus will activate the power of God and His anointing upon your life. Your willingness to answer the call of Jesus makes the difference, not your job or how many titles you have earned in life. It's not your position at that company or in the church. It's not how many cars you have parked in your driveway.

It's not how many children you have, it's not your experience in the ministry, it's not how good-looking you are, and it's not how many ministries you oversee. I can go on, and on, and on with this, but I want you to understand me very well. All these things are great to have and do, but they don't move God, and they don't release His power upon our lives. It's our willingness to follow Jesus that moves Him; it's when we're willing that we will be able to win a soul for Jesus!

The Bible gives us a clear picture here in Matthew 20:1-16, where Jesus likens the kingdom of heaven to a householder who had a vineyard and went out early in the morning at about 6:00 a.m. to hire laborers for his vineyard. He found some laborers, who **agreed** to work for him for one penny a day.

A penny here refers to a silver or gold coin of ancient Rome, first issued in the latter part of the third century BC. It fluctuated in value.

The Lord of the vineyard went out again about the third hour of the day (9:00 a.m.) and saw some workers standing idle in the marketplace. He said to them, "Go also and work, and whatever is right I will give you; so they went. Again, he went out the sixth and ninth hours (12:00 and 3:00 p.m.) and hired more laborers. Notice he kept going out, picturing our Lord and Savior Jesus Christ. The Bible says,

In the beginning God created the heaven and the earth. And the earth was without form and void; and darkness was upon the face of the deep. And the <u>Spirit of God moved upon the face of the waters.</u>
Genesis 1:1-2

The Spirit of God is still moving out on this earth today. He's looking for laborers in His harvest field. The Bible says,

After these things the Lord appointed other seventy also, and sent them two and two before His face into every city and place, whither He Himself would come. Therefore said He unto them, the harvest truly is great, but the labourers are few: pray ye therefore the Lord of the harvest, that He would send forth labourers into <u>His harvest</u>.
Luke 10:1-2

And about the eleventh hour (5:00 p.m.), the owner went out and found others standing idle. "Why have you guys been standing here all day idle?" He asked. They said to him, "Because no man has hired us." He told them, "Go also into my vineyard and whatever is right, that shall you receive. Now when the evening came, the lord of the vineyard said to his steward, "Call the laborers and pay them, beginning from the last unto the first."

Those who were hired about the eleventh hour received a penny each. When the first workers came, they expected to receive more, but they too received a penny each. When they received it, they murmured against the lord of the harvest saying, "We have worked all day and borne the burden and heat of the day, and you made us equal to these guys who worked just one hour."

The Lord of the harvest answered one of them, saying, "Friend, I did you no wrong; didn't you agree with me for a penny? Take what is yours and leave! I want to give this last guy as much as I gave you. Am I not allowed to do what I want with my own money? Are you envious because I am generous?" Jesus is asking you and me this same question today.

What I want you to get from this is a willingness to go after God and the work of God. Those laborers who were asked to go and work at 5:00 p.m. were willing. Because at that time it was already late, the day has nearly gone.

They could've said, "Sir, It's OK. This is not our time. Maybe we are just not lucky, or maybe it's because of our background that things are not really working for us. Maybe it's because of our sins that we are still unemployed. They could've given up on everything in life, but they didn't. Why? Because of their **willing-to-work attitude.**

Regardless of how late you entered the ministry or that local church, regardless of how little experience you may have, once you're willing to work for God, He is able to anoint you and raise you up and make you effective in your calling. Hallelujah!

God releases His anointing upon our lives when we become willing to answer the call to follow Jesus Christ, the Savior of this world. Don't ever think you don't and will never need Jesus. Remember, God's Word says we aren't sufficient in ourselves to think of anything. He is our sufficiency!

Not that we are sufficient of ourselves to think anything as of ourselves; but our sufficiency is of God; Who also hath made us able ministers of the new testament; not of the letter, but of the spirit: for the letter killeth, but the spirit giveth life.
2 Corinthians 3:5

We're not sufficient, or **enough,** in ourselves; our sufficiency or **ability** is of God, who has made us able ministers, or able servants, of the new covenant. See, God is able to make us sufficient and qualify us to do His work, only if we will be willing to follow Him wherever He is leading us. The Bible says the steps of the righteous or the good man are ordered of the Lord.

The steps of a good man are ordered by the LORD: and He delighteth in his way.
Psalm 37:23

Be Jesus-conscious

If you're going to be effective in your walk with Jesus, you must be conscious of Jesus and His kingdom. To be Jesus-conscious means to be fully aware of Jesus' existence; it means to have His **mind in your mind** continually!

Thou wilt keep him in perfect peace, <u>whose mind is stayed on thee</u>: Because he trusted in thee. Trust ye in the LORD for ever: for in the LORD JEHOVAH is everlasting strength.
Isaiah 26:3-4

You see, your consciousness of Jesus and His kingdom will determine your trust level. Many people, including Christians, don't have complete trust and faith in Jesus, because they aren't fully aware of Jesus' existence.

Your **trust and faith level** will determine your effectiveness in life as you walk with Jesus. Whenever your car's **oil level** becomes very low, it affects the ability of that car to take you to your destination. As oil is **very important** to the heart of a car (the engine), so is trust and faith important to your life.

Don't forget this: There will be storms in life as you follow Jesus down toward **New Jerusalem Street;** it's even evident that you will have to fall two or three times along that path toward New Jerusalem Street.

But that won't determine your arrival. If you hold the **mind of Jesus continually in your mind** as you travel, your trust and faith in Jesus will determine how you arrive with Him. Trust and faith is like a **light**; whenever you turn the light off, what you have is darkness. Where there's no trust and faith, then fear (darkness) comes in, and fear will bring you down in life as fast as an airplane that falls from the sky! Fear will destroy or weaken your defence system (your spirit); and when your defence system is weak, then you become open to the enemy, the devil, and his strategies.

Let this mind be in you, which was also in Christ Jesus: Who, being in the form of God, <u>thought it not robbery to be equal with</u>

<u>God</u>: But made Himself of no reputation, and took upon Him the form of a servant, and was made in the likeness of men: And being fashion as a man, he humble Himself, and became obedient unto death, even the death of the cross.
Philippians 2:5-8

Which mind is the apostle Paul talking about here? Is he talking about the mind of your dad, your president, or your manager? I don't think so. I believe he is talking about the mind-set of Jesus Christ, our Lord. You may ask why having the mind of Jesus is so important. It's important because Jesus walked this earth in **flesh, blood, bone, and body**. And He was subject to everything your physical body is subject to right now, but He didn't sin. He **triumphed and won!** Glory to God. Amen! The Bible says,

For we have <u>not</u> an high priest which cannot be touched with the feeling of our infirmities; but was in all points tempted like as we are, yet without sin.
Hebrews 4:15

We do have a high priest who was touched with the same feelings we have today, but thanks be to God, He didn't sin. Amen! He was also willing to do the will of His Father. That's what happens when you have Jesus' mind: it will enable you to be willing to do whatever He wants you to do.

Wherefore seeing we also are compassed about with so great a cloud of witnesses, let us lay aside every weight, and the sin which doth so easily beset us, and let us run with patience the race that is set before us, Looking unto Jesus the author and finisher of our faith; who for the joy that was set before Him endured the cross, despising the shame, and is set down at the right hand of the throne of God.
For consider Him that endured such contradiction of sinners against himself, lest ye be wearied and faith in your minds.
Hebrews 12:1-3

Looking unto Jesus will enable you to follow Jesus. How can you follow a person who's going to **New Jerusalem Street** when you are completely focused on **Unemployment Drive**? You will surely get lost. The same thing is happening today with many of God's people. They are saying, "I am Jesus' follower," but their minds are turned in another direction, in the direction of this world. Let me tell you, this world and its system is failing fast. The Bible says heaven and earth will pass away, but the Word of God (**Jesus**) will remain!

Heaven and earth shall pass away, but my words shall not pass away.
Matthew 24:35

Regardless of how many people are being laid off from their jobs, look to Jesus. Regardless of how much pain you're feeling in your body right now, look to Jesus. It doesn't matter what the news is saying, or what your bank account is showing; if you will keep your focus on Jesus and His word, you will win in life. Amen!

Now it came to pass, as they went, that he entered into a certain village: and a certain woman named Martha received him into her house. And she had a sister called Mary, which also sat at Jesus' feet, and heard His word. But Martha was cumbered about much serving, and came to Him, and said, Lord, dost thou not care that my sister hath left me to serve alone? Bid her therefore that she help me. And Jesus answered and said unto her, Martha, Martha, thou art careful and troubled about many things: But one thing is needful: and Mary hath chosen that good part, which shall not be taken away from her.
Luke 10:38-42

Jesus gives us a clear picture of two sisters here in this story. They both knew Him and followed Him through His ministry, but one of them lost her focus on Him. Jesus and His disciples were on their way to Jerusalem, and as they went, they entered a certain village where these two sisters lived. One of them, Martha, saw Him and recognized Him and opened up her home to them. But then she took her focus off of Jesus.

The moment this happened, she became distracted with much serving, and then anger started to creep in as well. You see what happens when you take your attention from Jesus. Life problems start to *manifest around* you when your eyes are no more on Jesus; but when your eyes and mind are completely focused on Jesus, even in the midst of problems, it will be as if they are no problems around you. Martha's sister, Mary, continued to look on Jesus, despite the confusion and distraction in their home. She wasn't moved at all by them. Instead, she sat down at His feet to hear what good news He came with. Hallelujah!

Jesus has good news of peace and prosperity with Him. That's why He said that whoever follows Him will never walk in the darkness;

Then spake Jesus again unto them, saying, I am the light of the world: he that followed me shall not walk in darkness, but shall have the light of life.

John 8:12

The Mind-set of James and John's Mother

Then came to him the mother of Zebedee's children with her sons, worshipping Him, and desiring a certain thing of Him. And He said unto her, what wilt thou? She saith unto Him, Grant that these my two sons may sit, the one on thy right hand, and the other on the left, in thy kingdom. But Jesus answered and said, Ye know not what ye ask. Are ye able to drink of the cup that I shall drink of, and to be baptized with the baptism that I am baptized with? They say unto Him, we are able. And He saith unto them, ye shall drink indeed of my cup, and be baptized with the baptism that I am baptized with: but to sit on my left, is not mine to give, <u>but it shall be given to them for whom it is prepared of my Father.</u>

And when the ten heard it, they were moved with indignation against the two brethren. But Jesus called them unto Him, and said, ye know that the princess of the Gentiles exercise dominion over them, and they that are great exercise authority upon them. But it shall not be so among you: <u>but whosoever will be great among you, let him be your minister; And whosoever will be chief among you, let him be your servant</u>: Even as the Son of man came not to be ministered unto, but to minister, and to give His life a ransom for many.
Matthew 20:20-28

Jesus is teaching us a great lesson here that I want to show you. I believe it's good to desire a higher place in life. I also believe it's good to desire positions in life. But your desire to follow Jesus should be greater, because as you follow Him, He will show you His way to becoming great in life. Everything we desire in this life has Jesus' way of going after it, and man's way of going after it:

There is a way which seemeth right unto a man, but the end thereof are the ways of death.
Proverbs 14:12

This is why it's very important to follow Jesus as you desire getting things and positions in life—because it's easy to lose focus on Jesus by being position-minded. Some people even create problems in the church because they're not given a certain position or because they're being denied some things in the church.

The same thing was going on here with James and John's mother. She had a different mind-set from what Jesus came to do here on earth. Jesus didn't come to set up a physical kingdom; He came to set up a spiritual kingdom in our hearts (Spirits):

And when He was demanded of the Pharisees, when the kingdom of God should come, He answered them and said, The kingdom of God cometh not with observation: Neither shall they say, Lo here! Or, lo there! For, behold, the kingdom of God is within you.
Luke 17:20-21

Many people under that dispensation couldn't understand what Jesus was up to, but, praise be to God, we can. Hallelujah! So this woman came to Jesus and said, "In your kingdom, please let my sons sit in places of honor next to you, one on your right, and the other on your left."

But Jesus said, "You don't know what you're asking. It's not mine to give, but it shall be given to them for whom it's prepared of my Father." When the other ten disciples heard this, they were angry, ready for a fight. Their Master had to call them together and explain plainly to them His mind-set about authority and places of honor. He said, "You know the people of this world exercise dominion over those they rule, but it shall not be so among you. Whoever wants to be great among you, let him be your minister and serve."

Jesus said we should desire to serve and minister; that's the God-way of going about this. By doing it His way, we keep our focus on Jesus as we go higher in life. Many people in positions today aren't serving, because they have their minds focused in another direction and not on Jesus. Regardless of where you live or work, don't be carried away by what others are saying but be **carried away by what Jesus is saying.** Keep your mind on Jesus Christ. He is Lord forever!

CHAPTER 3

WHAT DOES IT MEANS TO FOLLOW AND SERVE?

And Jesus answered them, saying, the hour is come, that the Son of man should be glorified. Verily, verily, I say unto you, Except a corn of wheat fall into the ground and die, it abideth alone: but if it die, it bringeth forth much fruit. He that loveth his life shall lose it; and he that hateth his life in this world shall keep it unto life eternal. If any man <u>serve Me,</u> let him <u>follow Me</u>; and where I am, there shall also my servant be: if any man serve me, <u>him will my Father honour.</u>

John 12:23-26

Jesus is again teaching us some kingdom principles of following Him. As we study together, I want to spend time talking about some key words in verse 26.

<u>SERVE:</u>
1. To do duty as a soldier.
2. To have definite use.
3. To answer the purpose.
4. To be useful; to render <u>active</u> service to a sovereign commander.
5. To perform the duties of position; an office.

The Bible shows us clearly that we are **soldiers** of the Lord. The Apostle Paul writes to the Christians in Ephesus:

Finally, my brethren, be strong in the Lord, and in the power of His might. Put on the whole armour of God that ye may be able to stand against the wiles of the devil. For we wrestle not against flesh and blood, but against principalities, against powers, against the rulers of the darkness of this world, against spiritual wickedness in high places. Wherefore take unto you the whole armour of God that ye may be able to withstand in the evil day, and having done all, to stand.
Stand therefore, having your loins girt about with truth, and having on the breastplate of righteousness; And your feet shod with the preparation of the gospel of peace; Above all, taking the shield of faith, wherewith ye shall be able to quench all the fiery darts of the wicked. And take the helmet of salvation, and the sword of the Spirit, which is the word of God: Praying always with all prayer and supplication in the Spirit, and watching thereunto with all perseverance and supplication for all saints; And for me, that utterance may be given unto me, that I may open my mouth boldly, to make known the mystery of the gospel, For which I am an ambassador in bonds: that therein I may speak boldly, as I ought to speak.
Ephesians 6:10-18

Paul also wrote to Timothy:

Thou therefore endure hardness, as a good soldier of Jesus Christ. No man that warreth entangled himself with the affairs of this life; that he may please him who hath chosen him to be a soldier.
2 Timothy 2:3-4

Jesus wants us to know that we're in warfare but not against flesh and blood. We are not fighting again human beings but against spiritual beings! We're engaged into active military action against spiritual forces at work against our families, jobs, school, and finances. We're also performing active military service for our Lord and Savior Jesus Christ. He's our sovereign commander in chief!

You know, in the United States Army, its OK to serve in **active** duty or in **reserve** units, but it is not that way in the Army of **Zion!** Within the Army of Zion, there are no reserves; everyone must perform **active service,** or you can't be a follower of Jesus Christ. In case you're a little confused with some words I am using here, let me make this clear to you: the Army of Zion is Jesus' army (the church). Zion is a spiritual kingdom where we live now and function spiritually. The Bible says,

You have not come to a mountain that can be touched and that is burning with fire; to darkness, and gloom and storm; to a trumpet blast or to such a voice speaking words that those who heard it begged that no further word be spoken to them, because they could not bear what was commanded: "If even an animal touches the mountain, it must be stoned to death. The sight was so terrifying that Moses said, "I am trembling with fear."

But you have come to Mount Zion, to the city of the living God, the heavenly Jerusalem. <u>You have come to thousands upon thousands of angels in joyful assembly</u>, to the church of the firstborn, whose names are written in heaven. You have come to God, the judge of all, to the spirits of the righteous made perfect, to Jesus the mediator of a new covenant, and to the sprinkled blood that speaks a better word than the blood of Abel.
Hebrews 12:18-24 (NIV).

No reserved services are allowed in Zion, where we serve — active service only! That's why I don't understand some Christians. When the news says there will be a storm on Sunday and we're expecting three inches of rain or snow, then some worship centers will close down for that day. I don't get it yet!

No one serving in the United States Army will say, "I am not going to work today because of three inches of snow or rain, especially when the commander in chief, the president, is planning to meet with them!

This is how you can really tell those who are serving as soldiers of Jesus Christ. Can you go to the meeting every Sunday, knowing that your sovereign Commander, Jesus Christ, is going to be present there that day? Understand this: when you were born again, from that day on, you were enrolled in the Army of Zion. You're no more your own; your life is hid in Christ Jesus. You are His!

I am crucified with Christ: nevertheless I live; yet not I, but Christ liveth in me: and the life which I now live in the flesh I live by the faith of the Son of God, who love me, and gave himself for me.
Galatians 2:20

Be Active in your service for God, and become a soldier of Jesus. Be certain about your service for Him on a daily basis. Know and answer the purpose for which you are here on this earth, be useful for God and His kingdom here on earth, always be ready to render active service and perform the duties of your calling and ministry. Be ready always to perform the duties of your office. God bless you.

FOLLOW:
1. **To go or come after; move behind in the same direction.**
2. **Watch closely, to observe, go alone, and obey.**
3. **To imitate or copy, keep up to date with; inform about something.**

Now let's take a closer look at the second phrase Jesus used here in John 12:26: "**Follow me**." When He said, "If any man serve me," He was referring to both males and females. If you are a teenager or an adult, He is talking to you. Whenever the Bible uses the word *man* in this way, it's talking about mankind, the species or the creation!

"If any man serve me, let him follow me" means let him come after me or move behind in the **same direction**. The only way you're going to arrive with Jesus is when you are going in the same direction as He is going—toward eternal life. It's not enough to say, "I am Jesus' follower" when you are not gathering together with God's people. When you study the life of Jesus as He walked this earth, you will find He went to the temple every time He was in Jerusalem (Luke 2:41-52; Matthew 21:12-13; Luke 13:10-13). Also, He was in the synagogue in almost every city He visited. A synagogue is a Jewish house of worship, an assembly or congregation of Jews for the purpose of religious worship. This was Jesus' custom when He walked this earth; so when He said, "Follow me," He was saying, "Do the same thing you see me do, and go the same places I am going."

He that is not with me is against me; and he that gathereth not scattereth abroad.
Matthew 12:30

I said this in the preceding chapter, but I want to reiterate it; when you follow Jesus Christ, you're commanded to always gather with other believers; this is going to make you effective in your Christian life. This instruction is for every Christian's benefit; every time you gather with other believers, your faith is strengthened. Why is this? It is because you will always meet with other Christians who are going through or who have gone through the same situation you're in right now. Your refusal to meet with others will make you ineffective in your walk with Jesus, which you don't want!

Sadly, most Christians still don't gather for worship. I asked myself one day this question: Why do most Christians refuse to gather with other believers? What's going on? Then the Spirit of God answered my question as I was meditating. He showed me two of the reasons for this.

1. Because they don't know God's Word, which says all Christians must gather together

…Not forsaking the assembling of ourselves together, as the manner of some is; but exhorting one another: and so much the more, as ye see the day approaching. For if we sin willfully after that we have received the knowledge of the truth, there remaineth no more sacrifice for sins, But a certain fearful looking for of judgment and fiery indignation, which shall devour the adversaries.
Hebrews 10:25-27

In verse 26, He's saying that if you don't gather together, then you're sinning willfully, because you have the truth already—right now! This is what He's really talking about if you study from the context, beginning from verse 19. He said we should **enter into God's presence** with boldness; then in verse 22, He said, **let's draw near** with a true heart. In verse 25, He's talking about gathering together, and He concludes by speaking of sinning willfully, which means not obeying!

2. Because they don't have Jesus always on their minds

If ye then be risen with Christ, seek those things which are above, where Christ sitteth on the right hand of God. Set your affection on things above, not on things on the earth. For ye are <u>dead and your life is hid with Christ in God</u>. When Christ, who is our life, shall appear, then shall ye also appear with him in glory.
Colossians 3:1-4

Many Christian have their jobs and problems on their minds more than they have Jesus and His kingdom on their minds. Consequently, they don't gather together. Know this: whatever you allow into your mind is what will control you. If you hold Jesus in your mind, I guarantee you, Jesus will control you!

<u>Watch Closely</u>

Jesus said, "If any man serve me, let him follow me" (John 12:26). We noted that "to follow" means to **watch closely** and **observe**, but what does this mean? In the book of 2 Kings beginning at the second chapter, we read that God was about to take Elijah— the fire prophet as we call him—Into heaven by a whirlwind. His servant Elisha walked with him. Also being a man of God, Elisha had an intuition about this whole situation.

As they walked from Gilgal, Elijah said to Elisha, "Tarry here, for the Lord has sent me to Bethel." Elisha replied, "As the Lord lives and as your soul lives, I won't leave you." When the two got to Bethel, Elijah the prophet said to Elisha, "Tarry here, for the Lord has sent me to Jericho." Elisha replied again that he would not leave Elijah. When the two got to Jericho, Elijah said to Elisha, "Tarry here, for the Lord has sent me to Jordan; but Elisha replied again, "As the Lord lives and as your soul lives, I won't leave you." Finally, the two came to the Jordan River, and Elijah the prophet took his mantle, wrapped it together, and smote the waters and the river was divided into two so that both of them walked on dry ground.

Now, what I want you to get from this story is this: As they both walked on dry ground, Elijah the prophet said to Elisha, "Ask what I shall do for you before I am taken from you." Elisha, his servant, said, "I pray, let a **double portion of your spirit be upon me**." Well, Elijah said, "You have asked a **hard** thing; nevertheless, **if you see me,** when I am taken from you, it shall be yours; but if not, it shall not be yours." I want to believe Elisha's eyes were open very wide at his master Elijah, as they both went down that road of Jordan!

And it came to pass, when the LORD would take up Elijah into heaven by a whirlwind that Elijah went with Elisha from Gilgal. And Elijah said unto Elisha, Tarry here, I pray thee; for the LORD hath sent me to Bethel. And Elisha said unto him, As the LORD liveth, and as thy soul liveth, I will not leave thee. So they when down to Bethel. And the sons of the prophets that were at Bethel came forth to Elisha, and said unto him, knowest thou that the LORD will take away thy master from thy head today? And he said, Yea, I know it; hold ye your peace.

And Elijah said unto him, Elisha, tarry here, I pray thee; for the LORD hath sent me to Jericho. And he said, As the LORD liveth, and as thy soul liveth, I will not leave thee. So they came to Jericho. And the sons of the prophets that were at Jericho came to Elisha, and said unto him, Knowest thou that the Lord will take away thy master from thy head today? And he answered, Yea, I know it; hold ye your peace. And Elijah said unto him, Tarry, I pray thee, here; for the LORD hath sent me to Jordan. And he said, As the LORD liveth, and as thy soul liveth, I will not leave thee. And they two went on.

And fifty men of the sons of the prophets went, and stood to view afar off: and they two stood by Jordan. And Elijah took his mantle, and wrapped it together, and smote the waters, and they were divided hither and thither, so that they two went over on dry ground.

And it came to pass, when they were gone over, that Elijah said unto Elisha, Ask what I shall do for thee, before I be taken away from thee. And Elisha said, I pray thee, let a double portion of thy spirit be upon me. And he said, Thou hast asked a hard thing: nevertheless, if thou see me when I am taken from thee, it shall be so unto thee; but if not, it shall not be so. And it came to pass, as they still went on, and talked, that, behold, there appeared a chariot of fire, and horses of fire, and parted them both asunder; and Elijah went up by a whirlwind into heaven. And Elisha saw it and he cried, My father, my father, the chariot of Israel and the horsemen thereof. And he saw him no more: and he took hold of his own clothes, and rent them in two pieces. He took up also the mantle of Elijah that fell from him, and went back, and stood by the bank of Jordan; And he took the mantle of Elijah that fell from him, and smote the waters, and said, Where is the LORD God of Elijah? And when he also had smitten the waters, they parted hither and thither: and Elisha went over.

2 Kings 2:1-14

In other words, Elijah was saying, "Watch me closely, because you have just asked a **hard** thing; so now you have work to do." Let me tell you, folks, nothing comes easy in this world, especially those things that come from the realm of the spirit. It will take your persistence; it will take hard work! When Jesus says, "Follow Me," He's not saying follow like a kid will follow his parents to the grocery store; for you know and I know that if you're walking your kids and your attention is not on them, they will probably hit their head against a light pole or against a stop sign pole along the road.

Why is that? It's because they don't pay attention when they walk. They just walk because they have legs to walk on and because they're seeing others walking. But, you see, we don't follow Jesus like that. We're commanded to follow with our eyes and minds on Jesus. If you can do that, I guarantee that you will have what you desire and you will arrive with Jesus in the New Jerusalem. Hallelujah!

Obedience

Obedience must be one of those factors in your mind as your follow Jesus, because there is no genuine follower who doesn't obey. You will be ineffective in your walk with Jesus if you refuse to obey when He talks. You will not be able to magnify your office as a soldier of Jesus Christ if you don't obey when your **sovereign commander in chief** talks to you.

Let me walk you through a few scriptures in God's Word and show you some of God's people who walked with Him. We will see what their obedience level was like—whether it was high or low or at zero.

Now the LORD <u>had said</u> unto Abram, Get thee out of thy country, and from thy kindred, and from thy father's house, unto a land that I will shew thee: And I will make of thee a great nation, and I will bless thee, and make thy name great; and thou shalt be a blessing: And I will bless them that bless thee, and curse him that curseth thee: and in thee shall all families of the earth be blessed.

So Abram departed, as the LORD had spoken unto him; and Lot went with him: and Abram was seventy and five years old when he departed out of Haran. And Abram took Sarai his wife, and Lot his brother's son, and all their substance that they had gathered, and the souls that they had gotten in Haran; and they went forth to go into the land of Canaan; and into the land of Canaan thy came.
Genesis 12:1-5

God had appeared to Abram, who was later called Abraham. God told him to leave his country, his father's house, and his relatives and go to a land that God would show him. You know and I know this is not that easy to do. Can you imagine encountering a person you haven't seen before who tells you to go to a place you haven't been before, and without any direction or roadmap to take along with you? But the Bible says that Abraham obeyed, and he went.

By <u>*faith*</u> *Abraham, when he was called to go out into a place which he should after receive for an inheritance, <u>obeyed</u>; and he*

went out, not knowing whither he went. By faith he sojourned in the land of promise, as in a strange country, dwelling in tabernacles with Isaac and Jacob, the heirs with him of the same promise.
Hebrew 11:8-9

Now get this: The Bible says Abraham did it by faith. He trusted in that voice that he heard from God, and he went forth with his family. Now, one of the reasons many of God's people don't obey Him is that they don't have any **trust and faith** in Him, and that's why their **minds** are not on Him. You must trust and have faith in God first in order to keep your mind on Him or in order to keep Him in your mind (Isaiah 26:3).

A few years later, the Bible says that Abraham had a kid who was called Isaac. God had made a covenant with Abraham to bless him and his seed after him. So the covenant lived on and was still **active,** even after Abraham died. The Bible says one day there was a famine in the land where Isaac dwelled, and Isaac decided to leave that land and go to a place where there was no famine; but something remarkable happened that I want to show you.

And there was a famine in the land, beside the first famine that was in the days of Abraham. And Isaac went unto Abimelech king of the Philistines unto Gerar. And the LORD appeared unto him, and said, Go not down into Egypt; dwell in the land which I shall tell thee of: sojourn in this land, and I will be with thee, and will bless thee; for unto thee, and unto thy seed, I will give all these countries, and I will perform the oath which I sware unto Abraham thy father; And I will make thy seed to multiply as the stars of heaven, and will give unto thy seed all these countries; and in thy seed shall all the nations of the earth be blessed; Because that Abraham <u>obeyed my voice</u>, and kept my charge, my commandments, my statutes, and my laws.
Genesis 26:1-5

The Bible says that we serve a God who is called Wonderful, Counselor, the mighty God, the everlasting Father, the Prince of peace! In other words He is the **Extraordinary Strategy** (Isaiah

9:6)! God's Word says that there was also a famine during the days of Isaac's father Abraham. At that time Abraham left and went into Egypt, where there was no famine. This was OK for Abraham as far as God was concerned.

But now there was another famine during the days of Isaac. Let me tell you this: There will always be trying and testing times wherever you live, but once God is with you, it doesn't matter where you live. He is still able to prepare a table before you in the presence of your enemies (Psalm 23:5). Amen! The Bible say that before Isaac could leave, God appeared to him and said to him, "Isaac, sojourn in this land, for I will be with you and will bless you, and I will give unto you and your seed all of these countries, and I will perform the oath which I swear unto your father Abraham." God made this promise because Abraham **obeyed His voice.** How simple this is. You want to tell me that God is doing all of these things to this one man, because of his father's obedience to God? Oh, yes.

God is telling us the same thing today: that if we will obey His voice, He will do even greater things for us, because of the new covenant that was established by the blood of Jesus Christ. Amen! Your obedience to Jesus' word as you follow Him is very important.

Imitate and Copy

Jesus said, "If any man serve me, let him follow me"; that is, let him imitate, copy, and get informed about me. How is this going to be possible? One way I believe this becomes possible is when we get into God's Word and study it for ourselves and do His Word. Knowing God's Word is one thing; doing God's Word is another thing:

But we all, with open face beholding as in a glass the glory of the Lord, are changed into the same image from glory to glory, even as by the Spirit of the Lord.
2 Corinthians 3:18

The glass Paul is talking about here is the Word of God; it is the mirror of God. Looking into God's Word is like looking into a mirror. God's Word shows us what we really are. It shows us our real image, and our real image is Jesus Christ. So, the more we look, the more we are changed into the **same image (Jesus' Image)!**

Strive to practice the sayings or the words of Jesus, because your prosperity, peace, and divine health are tied to doing the words of Jesus. The Word of God is like a wrapped gift, and you don't know what's in a gift until you open it up. That's why the Bible says,

The unfolding of your words gives light; it gives understanding to the simple.
Psalm 119:130 (NIV)

Who opens the Word of God? You're the one who must open God's Word, by diligently searching through the Scriptures and continually staying in His presence or in the fellowship together with other Christians. Whenever you do what Jesus has said or what He is saying, then you're **unfolding** His Words in your life. And as you do this, the light that is **encapsulated** in Jesus' words will enlighten your life. However, you must continue to do this. Your application to the words of Jesus will determine the results you're going to get from it.

And why call ye me, Lord, Lord, and do not the things which I say? Whosoever cometh to me, and heareth my sayings and doeth them, I will shew you to whom he is like. He is like a man which built an house, and digged deep, and laid the foundation on a rock: and when the flood arose, the stream beat vehemently upon that house, and could not shake it: for it was founded upon a rock. But he that heareth, and doeth not, is like a man that <u>without a foundation</u> built an house upon the earth; against which the stream did beat vehemently, and immediately it fell; and the ruin of that house was great.
Luke 6:46-49

Here Jesus is stressing the importance of doing His Words. He's saying that it's not enough to come to Him and hear His words; coming to Jesus and hearing His words is like being a born-again

Christian, which is not enough. You must strive to establish yourself in the faith. Establishing yourself in the faith, or in Jesus, is your responsibility; it's what you must do to survive the storm of life. As you do this, you're like the man striving to build his house. And we know it's not easy to build; it's going to take diligence and effort.

Jesus said the man building his house dug deep and laid the foundation on a rock, meaning you must be diligent in your search and study of God's Word in order to build your life on a foundation in the words of Jesus. As you do this, you're establishing yourself in Him. Then, when the storms of life—sickness, poverty, pestilence, and all the other problems of life—come up against you, they will not be **able** to destroy your life because you're standing on the Word of God, which is Jesus Christ.

But if you don't do this, you will be like the other Christian who is with Jesus, hearing His words but is not doing the word; he's not striving to build his life on a foundation (the Word). That's why sometimes you hear of some Christian who was destroyed by the storm. Somebody will say he or she was a faithful Christian, so why is that happening to him, or why has that happened to her? Let me tell you, faithfully hearing the Word of God without faithfully doing it is **building without a foundation.** Let's see what happened to the Christians in Berea. Those who heard the Word in Berea were different from those in Thessalonica, because they heard God's words with a ready mind, and they **searched the scriptures daily.**

And the brethren immediately sent away Paul and Silas by night unto Berea: who coming thither when into the synagogue of the Jews. These were more noble than those in Thessalonica, in that they received the word with all readiness of mind, and searched the scriptures daily, whether those things were so. Therefore many of them believed; also of honorable women which were Greeks, and of men, not a few.

Acts 17:10-12

The more you search, the more you'll dig; the more you dig, the more you'll find revelation from God's Word, and you'll build on a solid foundation, which is Jesus and His words (Matthew 7:7). You need God's Word to survive in these last days, or your house will not stand when the storms come. All you really need is a word for your situation. Peter needed just a word when he wanted to walk on the water to Jesus:

And straightway Jesus constrained his disciples to get into a ship, and to go before him unto the other side, while he sent the multitudes away, he went up into a mountain apart to pray: and when the evening was come, he was there alone. But the ship was now in the midst of the sea, tossed with waves: for the wind was contrary. And in the fourth watch of the night Jesus went unto them, walking on the sea. And when the disciples saw him walking on the sea, they were troubled, saying, it is a spirit; and they cried out for fear. But straightway Jesus spake unto them, saying, be of good cheer; it is I; be not afraid.

And Peter answered Him and said, Lord, if it be thou, bid me come unto thee on the water. And he said, Come. And when Peter was come down out of the ship, he walked on the water, to go to Jesus. But when he saw the wind boisterous, he was afraid; and beginning to sink, he cried, saying, Lord, save me. And immediately Jesus stretched forth his hand, and caught him, and said unto him, O thou of little faith, wherefore didst thou doubt?
Matthew 14:22-31

The Bible says that at (3:00 a.m. Jesus came to His disciples, walking on the sea. They were afraid and thought He was a spirit, but Jesus said to them, "Be not afraid; it's I." When Peter heard that, he answered Him and said, "Lord if it's You, tell me to come to You on the water." And Jesus released one word: "Come." That's all Peter needed to walk on the water to Jesus. No wander the Bible says God's **Word** is quick and powerful:

For the word of God is quick, and powerful, and sharper than any two-edged sword, piercing even to the dividing asunder of soul and spirit, and of the joints and marrow, and is a discerner of the thoughts and intents of the heart.
Hebrews 4:12

How terrible it is to build without a foundation. That is building without thinking of the storms of life that will one day come. What are you going to do when the storm shows up? I tell you, Jesus says that the ruin of that house will be very great! But if you continue to study the Word by reading books and listening to messages about Jesus and His kingdom, I tell you, when the storm comes, you will stand through it, in Jesus' name. Amen!

According to the grace of God which is given unto me, as a wise master builder, I have laid the foundation, and another buildeth thereon. But let every man take heed how he buildeth thereupon. For other foundation can no man lay that is laid, which is Jesus Christ. Now if any man build upon this foundation gold, silver precious stones, wood, hay, stubble; Every man's work shall be make manifest: for the day shall declare it, because it shall be revealed by fire; and the fire shall try every man's work of what sort it is. If any man's work abide which he hath built thereupon, he shall receive a reward. If any man's work shall be burned, he shall suffer loss: but he himself shall be save; yet so as by fire.
1 Corinthians 3:10-15

The name of the LORD is a strong tower: the righteous runneth into it, and is safe.
Proverbs 18:10

I charge you to do the sayings of Jesus as you follow Him, and your life will never be the same. Amen!

CHAPTER 4

THE DIFFERENCE BETWEEN DAVID AND SAUL

I want to talk to you about the lives of two great men. These men followed God, and He used them for His purpose; but there were some differences between these men, because of their mind-set and their character. Having a right character as you follow Jesus is very important, for your character will either keep you on course or will take you off course.

James and John followed Jesus but with a **different heart or spirit.**

And it came to pass, when the time was come that He should be received up, he steadfastly set his face to go to Jerusalem, and sent messengers before His face: and they went, and entered into a village of Samaritans, to make ready for Him. And they did not receive Him, because His face was as though He would go to Jerusalem. And when His disciples James and John saw this, they said, Lord, wilt thou that we command fire to come down from heaven, and consume them, even as Elias did? But He turned, and rebuked them, and said, ye know not what manner of spirit ye are of. For the Son of man is not come to destroy men's lives, but to save them. And they went to another village.

Luke 9:51-56

Sometimes when we think we're really doing God a favor, we're not. That's because we can't do any better if we don't know better; so in our ignorance we oppose God many times without even knowing it. **Saul of Tarsus,** who later became the apostle Paul, worked against Jesus many times before his conversion; but he really didn't know that he was in opposition to God, until he was confronted by Jesus on the road to Damascus.

And Saul was consenting unto his death. And at that time there was a great persecution against the church which was at Jerusalem; and they were all scattered abroad throughout the regions of Judaea and Samaria, except the apostles. And devout men carried Stephen to his burial, and made great lamentation over him. As for Saul, he made havock of the church, entering into every house, and haling men and women committed them to prison.

Acts 8:1-3

And Saul, yet breathing out threatening and slaughter against the disciples of the Lord, went unto the high priest, And desired of him letters to Damascus to the synagogues, that if he found any of this way, whether they were men or women, he might bring them bound unto Jerusalem. And as he journeyed, he came near Damascus: and suddenly there shined round about him a light from heaven: And he fell to the earth, and heard a voice saying unto him, Saul, Saul, why persecutest thou me? And he said, Who art thou, Lord?

And the Lord said I am Jesus whom thou persecutest: it is hard for thee to kick against the pricks. And he trembling and astonished said, Lord, what wilt thou have me to do? And the Lord said unto him, Arise, and go into the city, and it shall be told thee what thou must do. And the men which journeyed with him stood speechless, hearing a voice, but seeing no man. And Saul arose from the earth; and when his eyes were opened, he saw no man: But they led him by the hand, and brought him into Damascus. And he was three days without sight and neither did eat nor drink.

Acts 9:1-9

This is Saul, who later became the great Apostle Paul. He had given approval to the death of Stephen. And after this, he didn't stop. The Bible says he was breathing out threats and slaughter against the disciples of the Lord and went to the high priest, desiring letters to go up to Damascus, that he may bring more Christians bound to Jerusalem.

But in essence Jesus said to him, "Saul, Saul, it's enough now. Why are you persecuting me." He recognized that the voice was from heaven and said, "Who art thou, Lord? And the voice said, "I am Jesus, whom you are persecuting." And it was just that one encounter that changed everything in his heart and mind about the body of Christ. In fact, he became part of the body of Christ and went out preaching Jesus Christ crucified. What a great God we serve. He's able to change a murderer's heart with just one encounter. That's all you need. One encounter with Jesus will break all the powers of the enemies upon your life. The same Jesus Saul had worked against for a long time because of religion was the same Jesus he now was working for. Everything was changed in just a few minutes. Hallelujah!

But what I want you to get is this: Saul of Tarsus thought he was doing God a favor because of his religious upbringing. He had thought for a long, long, time that this way was the right way—that anyone who was preaching in the name of Jesus must be stopped. It takes the power of God to break that religious thinking.

Now let's see what happened to Saul, the son of Kish, when he became king over Israel. Saul was a good man who loved his people and cared about them. In fact, his attention was so focused on his people that it drifted away from his commander in chief, God, the one who called him into the kingdom and made it possible for him to sit in authority over the nation of Israel. His mind was so much after the people he was leading and he cared so much about how they praised him and how many people he had around him that they became his primary concern.

As a result, he missed the real person, the God who anointed him king over the people. If you're going to be effective as you follow Jesus, your whole attention must be set on Him. Without doing this, you're not going to please Jesus; you will miss out on Him **big-time**!

Saul reigned one year; and when he had reigned two years over Israel, Saul chose him three thousand men of Israel; whereof two thousand were with Saul in Michmash and in mount Bethel, and a thousand were with Jonathan in Gibeah of Benjamin: and the rest of the people he sent every man to his tent. And Jonathan smote the garrison of the Philistines that was in Geba and the Philistines heard of it. And Saul blew the trumpet throughout all the land, saying, Let the Hebrews hear. And all Israel heard say that Saul had smitten a garrison of the Philistines and that Israel also was had in abomination with the Philistines. And the people were called together after Saul to Gilgal.

And the Philistines gathered themselves together to fight with Israel, thirty thousand chariots, and six thousand horsemen, and people as the sand which is on the sea shore in multitude: and they came up, and pitched in Michmash, eastward from Bethaven. When the men of Israel saw that they were in a strait, (for the people were distressed), then the people did hide themselves in caves, and in thickets, and in rocks, and in high places, and in pits. And some of the Hebrews went over Jordan to the land of Gad and Gilead. As for Saul, he was yet in Gilgal, and all the people followed him trembling. And he tarried seven days, according to the set time that Samuel had appointed: But Samuel came not to Gilgal; <u>and the people were scattered from him</u>. And Saul said; bring hither a burnt offering to me and peace offerings. And he offered the burnt offering.

And it came to pass, that as soon as he had made an end of offering the burnt offering, behold, Samuel came; and Saul went to meet him, that he might salute him. And Samuel said, what hast thou done? And Saul said, Because I saw that the <u>people were scattered from me,</u> and that thou camest not within the days appointed, and that the Philistines gathered themselves together at Michmash; Therefore said I, The Philistines will come down now upon me to Gilgal, and I have not made supplication unto the LORD: <u>I forced myself therefore,</u> and offered a burnt offering.

And Samuel said to Saul, Thou hast done foolishly: thou hast not kept the commandment of the LORD thy God, which he commanded thee, for now would the LORD have established thy

kingdom upon Israel for ever. But now thy kingdom shall not continue: the LORD hath sought him a man after his own heart, and the LORD hath commanded him to be captain over his people, because thou hast not kept that which the LORD commanded thee.
1 Samuel 13:1-14

Saul, the king of Israel, had reigned for just two years in his kingdom when he heard that the Philistines had gathered themselves together to fight against his people Israel. The Philistines were as numerous as the sand on the seashore. When the people of Israel saw that they were surrounded, they were distressed and hid themselves in caves, rocks, and high places. Saul was still in Gilgal at this time, waiting for the man of God, Samuel the prophet, to come to him within seven days, as Samuel had said.

But Samuel didn't show up till after the seven days that were appointed. The prophet was delayed for God's own reasons. Sometimes when you really expect God to show up, He doesn't. Why? Because His ways are not our ways, thanks be to God. The Bible says,

For the vision is yet for an appointed time, but at the end it shall speak, and not lie: though it tarry, wait for it; because it will surely come, it will not tarry.
Habakkuk 2:3

Jesus doesn't move on our time; we move on His time. He sometimes shows up when all hope seems to be gone. When society gives up on us, then Jesus shows up to take the mess. He loves the one who is in the mess, and He is able to make something good out of the mess. It was when Lazarus's body had begun to stink that Jesus said to take away the stone (John 11:39). Why? So that people would believe (verse 15).

When Samson give up on everything and thought that he was going to die of thirst, God created a hollow in the ground and caused water to come out for Samson in a place where it was not possible, naturally speaking, for anyone to get water. But with God all things are possible; and as you walk with Him, all things will be possible for you in Jesus' name. Amen!

And he found a new jawbone of an ass, and put forth his hand, and took it, and slew a thousand men therewith. And Samson said, with the jawbone of an ass, heaps upon heaps, with the jaw of an ass have I slain a thousand men. And it came to pass, when he had made an end of speaking, that he cast away the jawbone out of his hand, and called that place Ramathlehi.

And he was sore athirst, and called on the LORD, and said, Thou hast given this great deliverance into the hand of thy servant: and now shall I die for thirst, and fall into the hand of the uncircumcised? But God clave an hollow place that was in the jaw, and there came water there out; and when he had drunk, his spirit came again, and he revived; wherefore he called the name thereof Enhakkore, which is in Lehi unto this day.
Judges 15:15-19

God has His own ways of doing things. He works for no one. We work for Him, and He wants us to have faith in Him. Even if it seems like nothing is working, have faith in God; He will show up. Continue to keep your focus on Him. King Saul was people-minded more than he was anointing-minded. He was focused too much on the people around him. That's why he was confused when all the people started to leave him.

It is better to please God than to please the people you are leading, but you can't do this easily until you get your mind completely on Jesus. Sometimes this may cost you everything, including the people you are leading, but that's the right way to go. When you fall, Jesus will lift you up. His grace is sufficient for us and His strength is made perfect in our weakness (2 Corinthians 12:9). The people will always leave you. They may tell you, "I am with you till the end." They may say, "Even if everyone else leaves you, I won't." Please don't listen to that.

King Saul went ahead doing the very thing God told him not to do, and that cost him the kingdom. God had planned to establish his kingdom forever, but because he feared the people more than he feared God, God couldn't use him long, He couldn't establish his kingdom forever!

What about Jesus?

Jesus went through everything we are faced with today when He walked this earth. He could have become proud, He could have become selfish, He could have become people-minded, and He could have become disobedient to His heavenly Father; but He didn't. He chose to do what is right. That is why He is our perfect example forever! One day He was faced with a situation that was similar to what King Saul was faced with; let's see His reaction to that situation:

The day following, when the people which stood on the other side of the sea saw that there was none other boat there, save that one where into His disciples were entered, and that Jesus went not with His disciples into the boat, but that His disciples were gone away alone; (Howbeit there came other boats from Tiberias nigh unto the place where they did eat bread, after that the Lord had given thanks:) When the people therefore saw that Jesus was not there, neither His disciples, they also took shipping, and came to Capernaum, seeking for Jesus. And when they had found Him on the other side of the sea, they said unto Him, Rabbi, when camest thou hither?

Jesus answered them and said, Verily, verily, I say unto you, Ye seek me, not because ye saw the miracles, but because ye did eat of the loaves, and were filled. Labour not for the meat which perisheth, but for that meat which endureth unto everlasting life, which the Son of man shall give unto you: for him hath God the Father sealed, Then said they unto Him, what shall we do, that we might work the works of God? Jesus answered and said unto them, this is the work of God that ye believe on Him whom He hath sent. They said therefore unto Him, what sign shewest thou then, that we may see, and believe thee? What dost thou work?

Our fathers did eat manna in the desert; as it is written, He gave them bread from heaven to eat. Then Jesus said unto them, Verily, verily, I say unto you, Moses gave you not that bread from heaven; But my Father giveth you the true bread from heaven. For the bread of God is He which cometh down from heaven, and giveth life unto the world. Then said they unto him, Lord, evermore give us this bread.

And Jesus said unto them, I am the bread of life: he that cometh to me shall never hunger; and he that believeth on me shall never thirst. But I said unto you, that ye also have seen me, and believe not. All that the Father giveth me shall come to me; and him that cometh to me I will in no wise cast out. For I came down from heaven, not to do mine own will, but the will of Him that sent me. And this is the Father's will which hath sent me, that of all which He hath given me I should lose nothing, but should raise it up again at the last day. And this is the will of Him that sent me, that every one which seeth the Son, and believeth on Him, may have everlasting life: and I will raise him up at the last day.

The Jews then murmured at Him, because he said, I am the bread which came down from heaven. And they said, is not this Jesus, the son of Joseph, whose father and mother we know? How is it then that he saith, I came down from heaven? Jesus therefore answered and said unto them, Murmur not among yourselves. No man can come to me, except the Father which hath sent me draw him: and I will raise him up at the last day. It is written in the prophets and they shall be all taught of God. Every man therefore that hath heard, and hath learned of the Father, cometh unto me. Not that any man hath seen the Father, save he which is of God, he hath seen the Father.

Verily, verily, I say unto you, He that believeth on me hath everlasting life. I am that bread of life. Your fathers did eat manna in the wilderness, and are dead. This is the bread which cometh down from heaven, that a man may eat thereof, and not die. I am the living bread which came down from heaven: if any man eat of this bread, he shall live forever: and the bread that I will give is my flesh, which I will give for the life of the world.

The Jews therefore strove among themselves, saying, how can this man give us his flesh to eat? Then Jesus said unto them, Verily, verily I say unto you, except ye eat the flesh of the Son of man, and drink His blood, ye have no life in you. Whoso eateth my flesh, and drinketh my blood, hath eternal life; and I will raise him up at the last day. For my flesh is meat indeed and my blood is drink indeed. He that eateth my flesh, and drinketh my blood, dwelleth in me, and I in him. As the living Father hath sent me, and I live by the Father: so he that eateth me, even he shall live by me. This is that bread which came down from heaven: not as your fathers did eat manna, and are dead: he that eateth of this bread shall live forever. These things said He in the synagogue, as He taught in Capernaum.

Many therefore of His disciples, when they had heard this, said this is a hard saying; who can hear it? When Jesus knew in himself that His disciples murmured at it, He said unto them, doth this offend you? What and if ye shall see the Son of man ascend up where He was before? It is the Spirit that quickeneth; the flesh profiteth nothing: the words that I speak unto you, they are spirit, and they are life. But there are some of you that believe not. For Jesus knew from the beginning who they were that believed not, and who should betray Him. And He said therefore said I unto you, that no man can come unto me, except it were given unto him of my Father.

From that time many of His disciples went back, and walked no more with Him. Then said Jesus unto the twelve, Will ye also go away? Then Simon Peter answered Him, Lord, to whom shall we go? Thou hast the words of eternal life. And we believe and are sure that thou are that Christ, the Son of the living God. Jesus answered them, Have not I chosen you twelve, and one of you is a devil? He spake of Judas Iscariot the son of Simon: for he it was that should betray Him, being one of the twelve.

John 6:22-71

When Jesus walked this earth during His three years in ministry, He had many disciples, but many of them didn't believe in Him; they searched diligently for Him and were willing to forsake everything to follow Him. They didn't do that because of spiritual things but because of physical things. And do you know that Jesus was not moved by their presence. Why? Because He knew all men. He knew who believed in Him and who didn't, He had just preached a powerful message to them, but they didn't understand anything He was saying because their minds were focused on physical things only.

He said, "I am the bread that came down from heaven," but when they heard that, they murmured at Him and said, "Is this not Jesus, the son of Joseph, whose parents we know? How can He say, I came down from heaven? Jesus then went on, saying, "He that eats my flesh and drinks my blood dwells in me and I in him." They became even angrier with Him, and from that time on, many of His disciples went back and walked with Him no longer. But Jesus was not moved by that because He knew that no one comes to him except it is given to him of the Father (verse 65).

If you're really following Jesus, you will learn from Him. He said we should come unto Him, take His yoke, and learn from Him (Matthew 11:28-30). Don't learn from others' experiences in ministry; learn from Jesus' experience, by being a diligent student of His words. If you're in charge of a ministry and you're not experiencing the growth you desire, don't worry and cry about that; just know this: If God don't send people into your path, they won't come, for it is God who gives the increase. Sometimes if people are not coming as you wish, it's because of your **ability level**. Maybe you don't have the five-talents ability, or maybe you don't have the two-talents ability. Bur **remember, it's God who gives the increase**!

Who then is Paul, and who is Apollos, but ministers by whom ye believed, even as the Lord gave to every man? I have planted, Apollos watered; but God gave the increase. So then neither is he that planteth any thing, neither he that watereth; but God that giveth the increase. Now he that planteth and he that watereth are one: and every man shall receive his own reward according to his own labour. For we are labourers together with God: ye are God's husbandry, ye are God's building.
<div align="right">1 Corinthians 3:5-8</div>

For the kingdom of heaven is as a man travelling into a far country, who called his own servants, and delivered unto them his goods. And unto one he gave five talents, to another two, and to another

one; to every man according to his <u>several ability</u>; and straightway took his journey.
Matthew 25:14-15

All you need to do is keep your focus directly on Jesus, for He is our perfect example. He's the only one who will never fail you, and He will never leave you when you fall but will give you a second chance. Amen!

King Saul was given yet a second chance by God through the prophet Samuel, but still he didn't prove himself faithful. And I want you to understand something before we continue. Do you know that there were not many chances given under that dispensation? That is because the grace of Jesus Christ wasn't available at that time. So it was up to individuals to make wise choices with whatever chance they had at that time, but King Saul didn't. He completely missed out on God because of his mind-set.

Samuel also said unto Saul, the LORD sent me to anoint thee to be king over His people, over Israel: now therefore hearken thou unto the voice of the words of the LORD. Thus saith the LORD of hosts, I remember that which Amalek did to Israel, how he laid wait for him in the way, when he came up from Egypt. Now go and smite Amalek and utterly destroy all that they have, and spare them not; but slay both man and woman, infant and sucking, ox and sheep, camel and ass. And Saul gathered the people together, and numbered them in Telem, two hundred thousand footman, and ten thousand men of Judah.

And Saul came to a city of Amalek, and laid wait in the valley. And Saul said unto the Kenites, Go, depart, get you down from among the Amalekites, lest I destroy you with them: for ye shewed kindness to all the children of Israel, when they came up out of Egypt. So the Kenites departed from among the Amalekites. And Saul smote the Amalekites from Havilah until thou comest to Shur that is over against Egypt. And he took Agag the king of the Amalekites alive, and utterly destroyed all the people with the edge of the sword. But Saul and the people spared Agag, and the best of the sheep, and of the oxen, and of the fatlings, and the lambs, and

all that was good, and would not utterly destroy them: but everything that was vile and refuse, that they destroyed utterly.
1 Samuel 15:1-9

I believe God had a great plan for King Saul, but he couldn't keep up with God. If God is going to establish you, you must keep up with Him by following Him with all your heart, mind, and soul. God again sent the king on a second mission; he was given a completely clear instruction by God in verse 3 to utterly smite the Amalekites and destroy all that they had and spare them not, including men and women, children and infants, cattle and sheep, camels and donkeys.

But you won't believe this: King Saul turned again from following the command of God that was set before him, because he wanted to please the people he was leading. We have great Christian leaders in churches today who, like King Saul, oppose God many times because of money and the people they are leading. That is why there are so many divisions in churches today—because of money and people. There are many Christian leaders, who will fight over members today not because they love God so much, but because of money and people. If you really love God, you won't fight over God's people, because it's God who **gives the increase**, not you!

What causes fights and quarrels among you? Don't they come from your desires that battle within you? You desire but do not have, so you kill. You covet but you cannot get what you want, so you quarrel and fight. You do not have because you do not ask God. When you ask, you do not receive, because you ask with wrong motives, that you may spend what you get on your pleasures.
James 4:1-3 (NIV)

The Bible says we fight among ourselves because of our desires that are against God's Word. Many Christian leaders don't really depend on the anointing of God for increase; that's why they fight over members. If you really have faith in the anointing of God upon your life, you won't fight with other leaders for people or position.

The Difference between David and Saul

And it shall come to pass in that day, that his burden shall be taken away from off thy shoulder, and his yoke from off thy neck and the yoke shall be destroyed because of the anointing.
Isaiah 10:27

So, you see why we shouldn't fight among ourselves. The Bible says that the anointing have all powers, including yoke-destroying powers. A yoke is something that binds a person or animal to an object; a yoke represents bondage. When you realize that you have been bound by spiritual powers and you're anointed, you should be able to loose yourself from that bond because of the anointing of Jesus Christ upon your life. Amen!

When I used to play soccer, I loved playing in the defense. We had a saying that went like this: "Experienced players don't suffer or fight for position." This encouraged us to train harder so that we would be sure to have a place on the team. So, I always liked to train harder till I became stronger, especially in my legs, so that I would have a place in the defense every time there was a game. I never fought anyone to have a place in the defense. I depended on my practice, and I spent more time working out on my skills just to have a place on the team.

So what you need is to spend more time in the spirit with Jesus if you want to have more members or if you want to understand why you're not getting more members. Don't fight, don't break away, and don't cause conflicts among yourselves, for it is Jesus who gives the increase, not you! Another thing I want you to understand is this: We are all stewards in the kingdom of God. Those people we are leading are not *our* people. They are God's people, and at the end of the day, we all will give an account to our sovereign Commander in Chief, Jesus Christ.

King Saul numbered his soldiers together and got ready for battle against the Amalekites. He destroyed all the people there but spared King Agag and the best of the sheep, oxen, lambs, and the good things King Saul and his people took, but all those things that were not good he destroyed. God was angry with him and sent the prophet Samuel to him, but King Saul had left early in the morning for Carmel and set him up a monument there in his honor. He was ready to have a great celebration for the great work he had done.

Know this: just because people are pleased with you and they're glad that you're leading them doesn't mean you're doing what Jesus wants you to do as a soldier of the Lord. I believe doing what your Commander in Chief desires should be your primary focus, and not what the people desire. King Saul told Samuel he had carried out the Lord's instructions, but you know and I know he didn't. So Samuel said, "What's the reason for this bleating of sheep in my ear and the lowing of cattle that I hear?" He answered, "The soldiers brought the best part of the sheep and cattle from the Amalekites to sacrifice to the Lord."

Then Samuel said unto Saul, Stay, and I will tell thee what the LORD hath said to me this night. And he said unto him, say on. And Samuel said when thou wast little in thine own sight, wast thou not made the head of the tribes of Israel, and the LORD anointed thee king over Israel? And the LORD sent thee on a journey, and said, Go and utterly destroy the sinners the Amalekites, and fight against them until they be consumed. Wherefore then didst thou not obey the voice of the LORD, but didst fly upon the spoil, and didst evil in the sight of the LORD?

And Saul said unto Samuel, Yea, I have obeyed the voice of the LORD, and have gone the way which the LORD sent me, and have brought Agag the king of Amalek, and have utterly destroyed the Amalekites. But the people took of the spoil, sheep and oxen, the chief of the things which should have been utterly destroyed, to sacrifice unto the LORD thy God in Gilgal.

And Samuel said, Hath the LORD as great delight in burnt offerings and sacrifices, as in obeying the voice of the LORD? Behold, to obey is better than sacrifice, and to hearken than the fat of rams. For rebellion is as the sin of witchcraft and stubbornness is as iniquity and idolatry. Because thou hast rejected the word of the LORD, he hath also rejected thee from being king.

1 Samuel 15:16-23

God rejected Saul as king over Israel because he rejected the word of God. What a shock! This is what happens when we turn from following after the Word of God. It will cost you everything in life. I pray that we will be obedient continually to the will and command of Jesus Christ our Lord.

Let's take some time and look at the life of David after he was anointed to be king over Israel. First, I want you to read God's testimony of David compared to that of King Saul:

And when he had removed him, he raised up unto them David to be their king; to whom also he gave testimony, and said, I have found David the son of Jesse, a man after mine own heart, which shall fulfill all my will.

Acts 13:22

But now thy kingdom shall not continue: The LORD hath sought Him a man after His own heart, and the LORD hath commanded him to be captain over His people, because thou hast not <u>kept that which the LORD commanded thee</u>.

1 Samuel 13:14

Speaking of King Saul, God said,

It repenteth me that I have set up Saul to be king: for he is turned back from following me, and hath not performed my commandments. And it grieved Samuel; and he cried unto the LORD all night.

1 Samuel 15:11

But David had a different spirit or a different mind-set toward God and the people he was leading. He had faith in God from his youth, and he trusted in God for his deliverance. When he walked with God, his mind was set on God only. When many people around him didn't believe in him and didn't think he was fit and qualified for a certain job, he still had his faith and mind set on God.

Let me tell you this: there will always be people around you who will look down on you because of your status or because of your size or because of what you have or don't have; but as Paul the apostle told Timothy, his son in the faith, let no one look down on you because you're young, but always set an example for others in speech, conduct, love, faith, and purity. Amen!

Let no man despise thy youth; but be thou an example of the believers, in word, in conversation, in charity, in spirit, in faith, in purity.
1 Timothy 4:12

David started exercising his faith in God at around the ages of sixteen and seventeen. This is one of the reasons I believe he didn't struggle to trust God when he faced the champion of the Philistines, Goliath. He wasn't moved by what the people around him were saying—you're too small, you don't have any experience, you're proud. He wasn't moved by those things; he was moved by God's testimony concerning him and by what God had put upon him: the "anointing!" When everyone around him stood in fear, he stood in faith, looking to God, his deliverer. Amen!

He rehearsed the miracles of God in his life, and he rehearsed the promises of God concerning him. Even when he was before King Saul, who had no faith in God, he still rehearsed these same things.

And Saul said to David, Thou art not able to go against this Philistine to fight with him: for thou art but a youth, and he a man of war from his youth. And David said unto Saul, Thy servant kept his father's sheep, and there came a lion, and a bear, and took a lamb out of the flock: And I went out after him, and smote him, and delivered it out of his mouth: and when he arose against me, I caught him by his beard, and smote him, and slew him.

Thy servant slew both the lion and the bear: and this uncircumcised Philistine shall be as one of them, seeing he hath defied the armies of the living God. David said moreover, The LORD that delivered me out of the paw of the lion, and out of the paw of the bear, he will deliver me out of the hand of this Philistine. And Saul said unto David, Go, and the LORD be with thee.
1 Samuel 17:33-37

He defeated Goliath, not because he was stronger than the Philistine or not because he had military skills, but because he had his faith and mind on the God of Israel, the living God. He spoke words of faith when he faced Goliath. Whenever you're faced with challenging circumstances and demonic attacks, speak words of faith and not fear.

Then said David to the Philistine, Thou comest to me with a sword, and with a spear, and with a shield: but I come to thee in the name of the LORD of hosts, the God of the armies of Israel, whom thou hast defied. This day will the LORD deliver thee into mine hand; and I will smite thee, and take thine head from thee; and I will give the carcases of the host of the Philistines this day unto the fowls of the air, and to the wild beasts of the earth; that all the earth may know that there is a God in Israel. And all this assembly shall know that the LORD saveth not with sword and spear: for the battle is the LORD'S and he will give you into our hands.
1 Samuel 17:45-47

One thing I learned from studying King David's life is that He always had faith in the anointing upon his life. When the people he was leading turned against him, he still looked to God for help and encouragement. One day he was faced with the similar situation King Saul was faced with. The Bible says all the people spoke of stoning him because they were grieved for their children. David was still able, in the midst of that situation, in the midst of death, to encourage himself in the Lord. He was a man after God's heart. Hallelujah!

And it came to pass, when David and his men were come to Ziklag on the third day, that the Amalekits had invaded the south, and Ziklag, and smitten Ziklag, and burned it with fire; And had taken the women captives, that were therein: they slew not any, either great or small, but carried them away, and went on their way.
So David and his men came to the city, and, behold, it was burned with fire; and their wives, and their sons, and their daughters, were taken captives. Then David and the people that were with

him lifted up their voice and wept, until they had no more power to weep. And David's two wives were taken captives, Ahinoam the Jezreelitess and Abigail the wife of Nabal the Carmelite. And David was greatly distressed; for the people spake of stoning him, because the soul of all the people was grieved, every man for his sons and for his daughters: but David encouraged himself in the LORD his God.
1 Samuel 30:1-6

Caleb and Joshua's Faith

After God brought Israel out of Egypt under Moses' leadership, He was ready to give them the land of Canaan He had long promised Abraham, Isaac, and Israel, a land that flowed with milk and honey. This land had everything in it to live a good life. But God couldn't give it to them without their participation. God is a faith God; so when He is leading us, He doesn't expect us to sit down and wait for whatever He has promised. He wants us to go lay hold of, or possess, what He has promised us. He told the children of Israel that every place where they set their feet would be theirs (Deuteronomy 11:24). So, it was up to them to make the move and take action, knowing that they would possess whatever land their feet touched because God almighty was with them.

That's faith. When you have prayed and then get up to act or speak, you're exercising faith in God. The Bible says God calls those things that are not as though they were (Romans 4:17). Faith is in the now. God wants us to be ready always to speak and act now! He told Moses to send out twelve men from the tribes of Israel to search out the land He had given to them.

And the LORD spake unto Moses, saying, Send thou men, that they may search the land of Canaan, which I give unto the children of Israel: of every tribe of their fathers shall ye send a man, everyone a ruler among them. And Moses by the commandment of the LORD sent them from the wilderness of Paran: <u>all those men were heads of the children of Israel.</u>
Numbers 13:1-3

The Difference between David and Saul

And Moses sent them to spy out the land of Canaan, and said unto them, Get you up this way southward, and go up into the mountain: And see the land, what it is; and the people that dwelled therein, whether they be strong or weak, few or many; And what the land is that they dwell in, whether it be good or bad; and what cities they be that they dwell in, whether there be wood therein, or not. And be ye of good courage, and bring of the fruit of the land. Now the time was the time of the first ripe grapes.

The place was called the brook Eshcol, because of the cluster of grapes which the children of Israel cut down from thence. And they returned from searching of the land after forty days. And they went and came to Moses, and to Aaron, and to all the congregation of the children of Israel, unto the wilderness of Paran, to Kadesh; and brought back word unto them, and unto the congregation, and shewed them the fruit of the land. And they told him, and said, we came unto the land whither thou sentest us, and surely it floweth with milk and honey; and this is the fruit of it. Nevertheless the people are strong that dwell in the land and the cities are walled, and very great: and moreover we saw the children of Anak there. The Amalekites dwell in the land of the south: and the Hittites, and the Jebusites, and the Amorites, dwell in the mountains: and the Canaanites dwell by the sea, and by the coast of Jordan.

And Caleb stilled the people before Moses, and said, Let us go up at once, and possess it; for we are well able to overcome it. But the men that went up with him said, We be not able to go up against the people; for they are stronger than we. <u>*And they brought up an evil report*</u> *of the land which they had searched unto the children of Israel, saying the land through which we have gone to search it, is a land that eateth up the inhabitants thereof; and all the people that we saw in it are men of a great stature. And there we saw the giants, the sons of Anak, which come of the giants: and we were in our own sight as grasshoppers, and so we were in their sight.*

<div align="right">Number 13:17-33</div>

Our God is a great God, His instructions are always clear, with detail, and to the point. He will never send you on a mission without clear, detailed instructions. He always makes sure you understand the mission before He releases you to accomplish it.

Here we see that God had given Moses clear, detailed instructions for His mission. God told him to send out twelve men from the tribes of Israel to go and **search out the land of Canaan** to see whether the people who lived there were **strong or weak, few or many**. What **kind of land** did they live in? Was it **good or bad**? What about the **towns they lived in**? Were they **unwalled or fortified**? How was the **soil**? Was it **fertile or poor**? Were there **trees** there or not?

Those were the instructions God gave to Moses for the twelve leaders of Israel. Those leaders were representatives of the tribes of Israel. They were responsible for the protection of their people. Whether they arrived safely in the land of Canaan or not was on them. That's why it was very important how they searched, what they said, and where they searched. God already knew the condition of the land of Canaan before sending out those men from the camp of Israel, but their obedience would prove their faith in Him.

They weren't to go to some other places where Moses didn't send them. The safe arrival of the people in the land of Canaan wasn't on God, and neither was it on Moses. God had told Moses to grant a certain amount of authority to those twelve leaders, by separating them from among the congregation of Israel.

The Bible says they went out and explored the land from Zin as far as Rehob, toward Lebo Hamath. Before I proceed, I want you to understand that those twelve men were commanded to bring back reports about the land of Canaan and the people who lived in the land. They weren't to come and say anything other than that. They weren't asked to give their recommendations.

The men came back and reported everything they saw in the land, including the fruit that was there. This wasn't a problem. Saying what you've seen is not a problem, but speaking contrary to, or against, what God has said is a problem. This crosses the line into another man's territory, so the speak.

That is just what they did; they crossed the line by doing what God didn't tell them to do and spoke against God. Every time you speak contrary to what God has said, you're speaking against God.

They said, "We're not able to go up against the people; they're stronger than we are. When they said that, the Bible declares that they brought up an evil report of the land they had searched; they saw themselves as grasshoppers in their own eyes. Why? Because they lost faith in God. Whenever you walk with God without faith, you will always see the negative rather than the positive.

Faith in God will always attract the positive; fear, on the other hand, will always attract the negative. We see this very thing with Jesus' disciples:

And the same day, when the even was come, he saith unto them, Let us pass over unto the other side. And when they had sent away the multitude; they took him even as he was in the ship. And there were also with Him other little ships. And there arose a great storm of wind, and the waves beat into the ship, so that it was now full. And he was in the hinder part of the ship, asleep on a pillow: and they awake Him, and say unto Him, Master, carest thou not that we perish? And He arose, and rebuked the wind, and said unto the sea, Peace be still. And the wind ceased, and there was a great calm. And he said unto them, why are ye so fearful? How is it that ye have no faith? And they feared, and said one to another, What manner of man is this, that even the wind and the sea obey Him?

Mark 4:35-41

You see what has happened: they all agreed and went; but when things weren't going well with them, they changed their minds about Jesus. They forgot what He said, and they said to Him, "Master, don't you care if we perish?" He had just told them a short time before, "Let's pass over to the other side," but because of fear, they couldn't **keep up with Jesus' word.** When you lose faith in Jesus, you lose the battle! The disciples suffered from the storm, not because Jesus was asleep in the hinder part of the ship, but because they lost faith and spoke contrary to what He had said. The same thing is happening today. Many of God's people are suffering from the storms of life because they have no faith in Jesus and because they're speaking contrary to what He has said.

Ten men cautioned against entering the Promised Land of Canaan because they lost faith in God and they spoke contrary to what He had said. But the Bible shows us two men from among the twelve who kept their faith in God. They came back with a good report. They kept on saying what God had said; they maintained their confession in the midst of the confusion around them. Why? Because they had a different spirit. They followed God with their whole heart. They were convinced that if God was with them they could take the land. They refused to be moved by what was happening around them.

Maintaining your confession of God's words will keep you alive in the storm. It will strengthen and encourage you. There will always be storms in life; but regardless of how strong the storms are, don't lose faith in God. Maintain your confession, and you will possess your inheritance. If you continue to hear and say what the news media are saying, you will soon believe what they're saying, because faith comes by hearing (Romans 10:17). The more you hear, the more you will speak; and the more you speak, the more you'll believe. That's why it's very important for you to hear God's Word continually and speak His words continually. This will build your faith in God. Amen!

CHAPTER 5

ALWAYS THINK BEFORE ACTING

Many people suffer needlessly in life because they react to life situations without first thinking through them or counting the cost. Before you make any decision in life, always ask yourself: What is going to come out of this? Is it going to build my faith or destroy it? Is it going to keep me in church or keep me out? Is it going to build me up physically or bring me down in life? Your answers to these questions are very important as you follow Jesus, because Jesus never did anything without first thinking or counting the cost. Remember that when Jesus walked this earth, He had a flesh, blood, and bone body. He was subject to everything our physical bodies are subject to today. He had a mind, and He could think. He got tired, hungry, and thirsty. Let's see what the Bible has to say about this subject.

For which of you, intending to build a tower, sitteth not down first, and counteth the cost, whether he have sufficient to finish it? Lest haply, after he hath laid the foundation, and is not able to finish it, all that behold it begin to mock him, Saying, this man began to build, and was not able to finish. Or what king, going to make war against another king, sitteth not down first, and consulteth whether he be able with ten thousand to meet him that cometh against him with twenty thousand? Or else, while the other is yet a great way off, he sendeth an ambassage, and desireth conditions of peace. So likewise, whosoever he be of you that forsaketh not all that he hath, he cannot be my disciple.

Luke 14:28-33

Here Jesus is talking about the cost of following Him, saying that those who will follow him must first forsake all and take up His cross and follow. But the important point I want to get across to you is in verse 28, where Jesus says, "Which of you who wants to build a tower won't first sit down and **count the cost** to see if you have enough money to complete the project?" And in verse 31, He asks, "Or what king who is going to war against another king won't first sit down and consider whether he is able with ten thousand men to oppose the one coming against him with twenty thousand?"

Counting is the activity of the mind; you can't count without using your mind. So, He is saying if you're going to undertake a project, you must first think and see if you're able to continue that project to completion. Starting a project is not really a problem, but ending that project is a challenge. It's always easy to start, but it's not easy to finish what you have started. That's why Jesus said the one who endures to the end shall be safe (Matthew 24:13). In other words, Jesus is saying you must first consider whether you're ready and able to continue what you want to start. I have seen a few people who got into the ministry without much training and experience. They rushed and started a church; but when things got a little harder and they couldn't continue what they had started, confusion and anger started to set in. Many people start a new job that interferes a little with their activities and schedule at church. They think things are going to get better in a few months, but they don't; and as time goes on, they completely stop coming to church!

This is what Jesus is talking about. If you'll first count the cost, it will be easy for you to get around and continue that project when problems arise. By counting the cost, you're using your mind; and the more you use your mind, the more you will expand your thinking capacity. And that is important because our minds control us. Whatever you allow into your mind will control you. Creflo Dollar once said, "The mind is like a cockpit in an aircraft." The cockpit is located in the forward fuselage of an aircraft and contains the flying controls, instrument panel, and seats of the pilot and copilot or flight crew. The cockpit door is always locked with a very strong lock, because whoever enters a cockpit is capable of controlling the aircraft wherever he or she desires. It is the same thing with the human mind. Whatever you allow to control your mind has the ability to control you.

Wherever you're working today or whatever you're studying today is a decision of your mind. It's what you allowed to enter your mind years ago. Too many people are making decisions today without thinking first. I want you to know the importance of thinking first before you act or before you speak, because whatever comes out of your mouth has the effect of destroying you, as well as the person you're talking to. The Bible says death and life are in the power of the tongue and they that love it shall eat the fruit thereof (Proverb 18:21). That's why we must always be very careful what we say, and, most important, we must think before we act or speak.

Brethren, be not children in understanding: <u>howbeit in malice be ye children</u>, but in <u>understanding be men.</u> In the law it is written, with men of other tongues and other lips will I speak unto this people; and yet for all that will they not hear me, saith the Lord.
1 Corinthians 14:20-21

The apostle Paul is saying something great here; he says to be men in understanding and not children. In other words, he is saying we should learn to use our minds more often than our mouths. In malice, we are to be children. The more often you use your mind, the more mature you become in life. Using your mind often makes you a man in understanding. Learn to meditate often. This will keep you from speaking foolish things, and it will enhance your thinking ability. Try to have a time set apart for just you. Find a very quiet place, and take some time to meditate. Studies have shown that often or long meditation keeps us from lots of problems and stress. The Bible also says that we should meditate upon the words of God and give ourselves wholly to them so that our progress may appear to all (1 Timothy 4:15). In meditation we use our mind and spirit.

Wherefore, my beloved brethren, let every man be swift to hear, slow to speak, slow to wrath: For the wrath of man worketh not the righteousness of God. Wherefore lay apart all filthiness and superfluity of naughtiness, and receive with meekness the engrafted word, which is able to save your souls.

James 1:19-21

Another reason it's important to be slow to speak is that it will limit and control your ability to get angry, for anger, or wrath, works not the righteousness of God but is the sin of the devil. James said be swift to hear. The more often you hear, the more often you put your mind to work; for as you hear words, those words are processed into the mind and create an image there. And when that image is perfected, it becomes a stronghold that will lead you either to promotion or destruction.

One reason the Bible says to be men in understanding is because men have the ability to control situations concerning their homes, but children can't. Children will never be able to do things at an adult level until they grow up. God also said to watch, stand fast in the faith, act like men, and be strong (1 Corinthians 16:13 ESV). So you see, men can be strong, but children cannot. God also said,

Therefore shall a man leave his father and his mother, and shall cleave unto his wife: and they shall be one flesh.

Genesis 2:24

Another thing men can do is leave their parents and cleave to their wives. Children can't do that; they have to grow up first. One reason God says that in malice to be children is that children are quick to forget wrongs done to them. If you are so evil that you hit a little child hard enough to hurt him, he will cry for some time. But the next day he will come back to you. Children are humble and lowly in heart.

But Jesus said, Suffer little children, and forbid them not, to come unto me: for of such is the kingdom of heaven.

Matthew 19:14

At the same time came the disciples unto Jesus, saying, who is the greatest in the kingdom of heaven? And Jesus called a little child unto him, and set him in the midst of them, And said, verily I say unto you, except ye be converted, and become as little children, ye shall not enter into the kingdom of heaven. Whosoever therefore shall humble himself as this little child, the same is greatest in the kingdom of heaven. And whoso shall receive one such little child in my name receiveth me.
Matthew 18:1-5

Exercise Your Senses

Of whom we have many things to say and hard to be uttered, <u>seeing ye are dull of hearing.</u> For when for the time ye ought to be teachers, ye have need that one teach you again which be the first principles of the oracles of God; and are become such as have need of milk, and not of strong meat. For every one that useth milk is unskilful in the word of righteousness: for he is a babe. But strong meat belongeth to them that are of full age, even those who by reason of use have their senses exercised to discern both good and evil.
Hebrews 5:11-14

Thinking before acting will save you from a lot of problems as you continue your walk with Jesus. Now I want to go through this part of Hebrews and see what God is saying concerning this subject. This letter to the Hebrews was written to Jewish Christians in Palestine. The author said they were **dull of hearing**; that was the first problem. The Bible says we should be quick to hearing, but they were dull of hearing. What a shock! This resulted in their slow learning, because they weren't exercising their minds enough. When they should have been teachers and leaders of the church and other Christians, they were still messing up and waiting to be taught the same things over and over again. They had become like those who have need of milk and not **strong meat**. They shouldn't have been at this level, but they had **become** as such. Why? Because of their lack of thinking and training of their senses.

God said they weren't ready for strong meat. They may have been ready for meat but not strong meat. There is meat, and there is **strong meat**. They weren't ready for the higher life in Christ Jesus. There is a lower life and there is a higher life in Jesus. The higher life is when you get to the **mountaintop** and start to see people with the eyes of Jesus. It's when you stop living a selfish life and start loving. It's when you stop excluding yourself from the gathering of the believers and start meeting for services on a regular basis. It's when you start winning souls for Jesus. Amen!

The Bible said everyone who uses milk is unskillful in the word of righteousness. Righteousness is the nature of God; it's the life of God. When you know you're righteous, sickness can't destroy your life. To be righteous means to be in right standing with God. Amen! Milk is for babies, but strong meat belongs to those who are of full age, even those who have learned to exercise or train their senses in the Word of God. As you study God's Word, you're training your senses to discern good from evil.

I beseech you therefore, brethren, by the mercies of God, that ye present your bodies a living sacrifice, holy, acceptable unto God, which is your reasonable service. And be not conformed to this world: but be ye transformed by the renewing of your mind, that ye may prove what is that good, and acceptable, and perfect, will of God.

Romans 12:1-2

When we were born again, we were translated from the kingdom of darkness of this world into the kingdom of Jesus Christ. As such, we should no longer act in accordance with this world or the system of this world. That's why James 1:19 says we should be swift to hear and slow to speak or act. As you do this, you're not acting according to this world. The Bible also says we should be transformed by the renewing of our minds. The only way I believe we can do this is by thinking through God's words, by studying and meditating on the Scriptures continually. As we do this, we will be able to prove what is that good will, acceptable will, and perfect will of God.

There is a good will of God, an acceptable will of God, and a perfect will of God, but reaching these levels requires your diligent study and exercising your senses through God's Word. Many Christians know His **good will**—that God gave His only begotten Son.

For God so loved the world, that he gave His only begotten Son, that whosoever believeth in Him should not perish, but have everlasting life. For God sent not his Son into the world to condemn the world; but that the world through Him might be saved.
John 3:16-17

There is also His **acceptable will**—that all Christians everywhere lift up holy hands and worship God in spirit and in truth, for God is a spirit.

I will therefore that men pray everywhere, lifting up holy hands, without wrath and doubting.
1 Timothy 2:8

But the hour cometh and now is, when the true worshippers shall worship the Father in spirit and in truth: for the Father seeketh such to worship him. God is a spirit: and they that worship Him must worship Him in spirit and in truth.
John 4:23-24

And there is His **perfect will**: God cannot lie, He cannot change His mind; He will remain the same forever, and in Him is light!

In hope of eternal life, which God, that cannot lie, promised before the world began.
Titus 1:2

...God is not a man that He should lie; neither the son of man that He should repent: hath He said, and shall he not do it? Or hath He spoken, and shall He not make it good?
Numbers 23:19

... Jesus Christ the same yesterday, and today, and forever.
Hebrews 13:8

This then is the message which we have heard of Him, and declare unto you, that God is light, and in Him is no darkness at all.
1 John 1:5

So you see, there are stages in the life of Jesus. As you follow Him continually, you're going to mature and grow to these stages. Amen! Now, let's look at some more scriptures to see how Jesus dealt more with this subject.

And when they were come to Capernaum, they that received tribute money came to Peter, and said, doth not your master pay tribute? He saith, yes. And when he was come into the house, Jesus prevented him, saying, <u>What thinkest thou, Simon</u>? Of whom do the kings of the earth take custom or tribute? Of their own children, or of strangers? Peter saith unto Him, Of strangers. Jesus saith unto him, Then are the children free. Notwithstanding, lest we should offend them, go thou to the sea, and cast an hook, and take up the fish that first cometh up; and when thou hast opened his mouth, thou shalt find a piece of money: that take, and give unto them for me and thee.
Matthew 17:24-27

Here we see Jesus asking Peter a question. He was also training him how to use his mind or how to think first before acting. They had just entered Capernaum, and one of the temple tax collectors came to Peter and asked, "Doesn't your teacher pay tax?" Peter replied, "Sure He does." But when Peter got into the house, Jesus had already perceived what had happened outside, and He asked Peter, "What do you think? From whom do the kings of the earth collect duty and taxes—from their own children or from strangers?

In order to answer Jesus' question, Peter had to use his mind. That's the main reason the question was asked of him. Jesus already knew the answer; so He wasn't asking to learn the answer. He was giving His disciple the chance to use his mind; He was training

Peter. Remember this, Jesus used every situation to teach His disciples, whether they were walking, sitting, or praying. That's why He is a master teacher. Amen! So Peter answered, "From strangers," and Jesus said, "Then the children are exempt, but so that we may not cause offense, go to the lake and throw out your line." And when Peter obeyed, you know what happened: he was able to pay his tax and Jesus' too. Amen!

The Woman Caught in Adultery

Jesus went unto the Mount of Olives. And early in the morning He came again into the temple, and all the people came unto Him; and He sat down, and taught them. And the scribes and Pharisees brought unto Him a woman taken in adultery; and when they had set her in the midst, they say unto Him, Master, this woman was taken in adultery, in the very act. Now Moses in the law commanded us, that such should be stoned: but what sayest thou? This they said, tempting Him that they might have to accuse Him. But Jesus stooped down, and with His finger wrote on the ground, as though He heard them not.

So when they continued asking Him, He lifted up Himself, and said unto them, he that is without sin among you, let him first cast a stone at her. And again He stooped down, and wrote on the ground. And they which heard it, being convicted by their own conscience, went out one by one, beginning at the eldest, even unto the last: and Jesus was left alone, and the woman standing in the midst. When Jesus had lifted up Himself, and saw none but the woman, He said unto her, Woman, where are those thine accusers? Hath no man condemned thee? She said, No man Lord. And Jesus said unto her, Neither do I condemn thee: go, and sin no more.

John 8:1-11

We are still on this subject of thinking before you speak or act. I want you to see again how Jesus dealt with situations that came His way. Here He is at the temple teaching, and the scribes and Pharisees brought to him a woman who had been caught in the act of adultery. They set her in the midst of the people; then, tempting Jesus, they said to Him, "Teacher, this woman was caught in the very act of adultery. The Law of Moses says to stone her. What do you say?"

Now remember, they were trying to trap Jesus into saying something they could use against Him. He had been teaching that He didn't come to destroy the law; so they wanted to see if Jesus was going to use His authority against the law by commanding that this woman shouldn't be stoned, seeing that she was caught in the very act.

Think not that I am come to destroy the law, or the prophets: I am not come to destroy, but to fulfill. For verily I say unto you, till heaven and earth pass, one jot or one tittle shall in no wise pass from the law, till all be fulfilled.
Matthew 5:17-18

Also, He had been preaching, that the Son of Man didn't come to destroy people's lives but to save them; so they wanted to see if Jesus would contradict His own word by commanding that this woman be stoned. Then, perhaps, I believe, they would had called Him a fake prophet.

For the Son of man is not come to destroy men's lives, but to save them. And they went to another village.
Luke 9:51-56

For God so loved the world, that He gave His only begotten Son, that whosoever believeth in Him should not perish, but have everlasting life. For God sent not His son into the world to condemn the world; but that the world through Him might be saved.
John 3:16-17

But Jesus, knowing more and better then all of the religious leaders of His day and ours, couldn't be trapped like that. The Bible says He didn't need anyone to testify concerning man, for He Himself knew what was in man (John 2:25). Jesus already knew what to say before these people came to Him, but I want you to see what His reaction was to their question: Jesus stooped down and wrote in the dust with his finger as though He had not heard them.

What was Jesus doing when He was writing on the ground? I believe He took some time thinking when or how to answer them. Now, don't tell me He didn't use His mind during that time when He stooped down. You may ask me why He did that. One of the reasons I believe he did that was to give His disciples and every one of us an example to follow. Remember, He was teaching before the scribes and Pharisees came up to Him, and, as I said previously, Jesus used every situation He was faced with to teach a lesson.

So He wasn't thinking just because He didn't know what to say but because He is a teacher, and He had something extra to teach on that day. He was showing us how to deal with such situations when we face them. He was letting us know that it is better to think and pray for more spiritual insight before making a decision. Amen!

The Bible gives us another interesting incident about Jesus and His disciples at the Passover festival in Jerusalem. Let's see what happened.

Now before the feast of the Passover, when Jesus knew that His hour was come that He should depart out of this world unto the Father, having loved His own which were in the world, <u>He loved them unto the end.</u> And supper being ended, the devil having now put into the heart of Judas Iscariot, Simon's son, to betray Him; Jesus knowing that the Father had given all things into His hands, and that He was come from God, and went to God; He riseth from supper, and laid aside His garments; and took a towel, and girded Himself

After that he poureth water into a bason, and began to wash the disciples' feet, and to wipe them with the towel wherewith He was girded. Then cometh He to Simon Peter: and Peter saith unto Him, Lord, dost thou wash my feet? Jesus answered and said unto him, What I do thou knowest not now; but thou shalt know hereafter. Peter saith unto Him, Thou shalt never wash my feet. Jesus answered him, If I wash thee not, thou hast no part with me. Simon Peter saith unto Him, Lord, not my feet only, but also my hands and my head. Jesus saith to him, He that is washed needeth not save to wash his feet, but is clean every whit: and ye are clean, but not all, for He knew who should betray Him; therefore said He, Ye are not all clean.

So after He had washed their feet, and had taken His garments, and was set down again, He said unto them, Know ye what I have done to you? Ye call me Master and Lord: and ye say well; for so I am. If I then, your Lord and Master, have washed your feet; ye also ought to wash one another's feet. For I have given you an example that ye should do as I have done to you. Verily, verily I say unto you, the servant is not greater than His lord; neither he that is sent greater than he that sent him. <u>If ye know these things, happy are ye if ye do them.</u>

John 13:1-17

Jesus was in Jerusalem at the Passover; and while the evening meal was in progress, He got up from the meal, took off his outer clothing, and wrapped a towel around His waist. He then poured water into a basin and started to wash His disciples' feet, drying them with the towel that was wrapped around Him. What do you think made Jesus do what He did? Well, in verse 15, He said, "I have given you an example that you should do as I have done to you." As He was doing this, He was also teaching His disciples a lesson—to do to others as He had done to them.

This is one of the reasons Jesus came—to show us what God is like and what He desires to do on this earth. Hallelujah! Regarding the woman caught in adultery, the Bible says her accusers kept demanding an answer from Jesus, because they thought He didn't know what to say. So He stood up and said, "All right, but let the one who has never sinned throw the first stone at her!" Then He stooped down again and wrote in the dust. When her accusers heard this, they slipped away one by one, beginning with the oldest. What a shock!

Then Jesus stood up again and said to the woman, "Where are your accusers? Didn't even one of them condemn you?" "No, Lord," she said. Jesus then said to her, "Neither do I. Go and sin no more." Thank God for Jesus, who will not condemn us when we sin but will always make a way of escape for us when we're tempted (1 Corinthians 10:13). Amen!

Woman, Where Are Your Accusers?

One thing I want you to understand as you continue your walk with Jesus is this: learn not to accuse people who are not as strong or holy as you are. Remember, we are living this Christian life, not by our own works, but by the grace of God. We are not perfect but striving toward perfection. Always learn to pray for your fellow Christians, because we all make mistakes. Another reason you should always pray for your fellow Christians is that we all needs prayer. Just because you're active today in prayer meetings and Sunday services doesn't mean you have arrived. You will one day need more prayers when you're going through life problems; so learn to pray for people and not talk about them. Remember, too, that not all people have faith.

Finally, brethren, pray for us, that the word of the Lord may have free course, and be glorified, even as it is with you: And that we may be delivered from unreasonable and wicked men: for all men have not faith. But the Lord is faithful, who shall stablish you, and keep you from evil.
2 Thessalonians 3:1-3

Judge not, that ye be not judged. For with what judgment ye judge, ye shall be judged: and with what measure ye mete, it shall be measured to you again. And why beholdest thou the mote that is in thy brother's eye, but considerest not the beam that is in thine own eye? Or how wilt thou say to thy brother, Let me pull out the mote out of thine eye; and, behold, a beam is in thine own eye? Thou hypocrite, first cast out the beam out of thine own eye; and then shalt thou see clearly to cast out the mote out of thy brother's eye.
Matthew 7:1-5

Jesus teaches us some very important principles about life and how to deal with people. He said the very first thing we should not do is to judge others. As a result, we won't be judged, for in the same way we judge others, we will be judged. In other words, He was saying we shouldn't stand back and point fingers at someone else's wrongdoing; rather, we should first clean up ourselves, because we may have more wrong in us than the one we're pointing to. Wow! So you see why we all need one another—because we all have problems. No one is good, but by God's grace we're trying to live a good life. That's why we must always pray for one another.

Confess your <u>faults one to another</u>, and pray one for another, that ye may be healed. The effectual fervent prayer of a righteous man availeth much.

James 5:16

God said we should confess our faults to one another and pray for one another, but this instruction is not really working today in the body of Christ. This is because many people are afraid that others will just hear their faults and look down on them or accuse them, rather than pray for them. This is one of the reasons many Christians are sick in the body of Christ today, for until we confess our faults, that issue won't be dealt with specifically through prayer, and we won't be healed. There are some demons that won't go away with just a single person praying, but they will go away with more prayers!

Every person is responsible to pray for others, and if we all, in fact, were praying for one another rather then accusing one another, there would be more miracles and more answers to prayers. Jesus said to pray for one another that we might be healed. I have a responsibility to pray for other Christians, and so do you. Your maturity is determined by how many people you are praying for, and your immaturity is revealed by how few people you're praying for and how many people you're accusing every day!

It's not how many years you have been a Christian or been in that local church that matters; it's how well you're taking care of God's people around you. Jesus said, if we do this, we show that we truly love Him.

So when they had dined, Jesus saith to Simon Peter, Simon, son of Jonas, lovest thou me more than these? He saith unto Him, Yea, Lord; thou knowest that I love thee. He saith unto him, <u>Feed my lambs</u>. He saith to him again the second time, Simon, son of Jonas, lovest thou me? He saith unto Him, Yea, Lord; thou knowest that I love thee. He saith unto him, <u>Feed my sheep</u>. He saith unto him the third time, Simon, son of Jonas, lovest thou me? Peter was grieved because He said unto him the third time, Lovest thou me? And he said unto Him, Lord, thou knowest all things; thou knowest that I love thee. Jesus saith unto him, <u>Feed my sheep</u>.
John 21:15-17

Jesus asked the woman caught in adultery, where her accusers were (John 8:10). I believe one reason Jesus asked her that question was not simply because He wanted to make the statement He made in verse 11 but because He was concerned about her accusers, just as He is concerned about your accusers. You may ask why this is. It is because He wants everyone to be saved. Jesus' purpose for coming into this world was that everyone should be saved. He loves even the sinners; so it didn't bring joy to His heart because all her accusers left. They all had sin in them, and they all went away with their sins! The same thing is happening today. It's still Jesus' desire for everyone to be saved, including those who condemn others.

If you're reading this book, and you know your number one job is to accuse people and look down on them, I want you to know that Jesus loves you and wants you to be saved now! You might say, "Well, I am a Christian, and I am already saved," but you still need to be saved. Hear what the Spirit of God told me one day as I was meditating. He said, "Do you know there are two places of salvation in a man? The first place is in his spirit, and the second is in his mind!"

Receiving Jesus Christ into your life, or your spirit, qualifies you for the kingdom of God; it makes you one with Christ. But if that is all there is to it, then very soon you would lose your salvation because your mind is not renewed or saved the moment you receive Jesus Christ into your heart. You have to get your mind renewed through God's words. Many Christians don't walk in love, and many look down on others and accuse others because their minds are not being controlled by God's words. To think like Jesus, your mind must be saved. To walk like Jesus, your mind must be renewed, for that's the only way you're going to know the good, acceptable, and perfect will of God (Romans 12:2).

CHAPTER 6
SUBMIT YOURSELF TO GOD

Except the LORD <u>build</u> the house, they labour in vain that build it: except the LORD keep the city, the watchman waketh but in vain. It is vain for you to rise up early, to sit up late, to eat the bread of sorrows: for so he giveth His beloved sleep.
Psalm 127:1-2

One way you can enhance your walk with Jesus is to learn to submit your will to His will. Allow Him to have control over your life; allow the Spirit of God to lead you as you follow. Because you don't know the street you are traveling on and have never been this way before, you must submit to Him.

And Joshua rose early in the morning; and they removed from Shittim, and came to Jordan, he and all the children of Israel, and lodged there before they passed over. And it came to pass after three days, that the officers went through the host; And they commanded the people, saying, When ye see the ark of the covenant of the LORD your God, and the priests the Levites bearing it, then ye shall remove from your place, and go after it. Yet there shall be a space between you and it, about two thousand cubits by measure: come not near unto it that ye may know the way by which ye must go: for ye have not passed this way heretofore.
Joshua 3:1-4

God was leading the children of Israel into the land He had promised them, but they had never been that way before. God was willing to lead them into the Promised Land, but they had to submit their will to Him in order to possess their inheritance. Their leader Joshua had commanded them, saying, "Whenever you see the ark of the covenant of God, and the priests carrying it, you're to move from your positions and follow it; then you'll know which way to go."

That was their instructions: they were to **leave their positions and follow the ark**. They were also commanded to keep a space of about two thousand cubits between them and the ark. Before I continue, I want us to look at the word *submit*. It has two basic meanings:

1. To give over or yield to the power or authority of another.
2. To subject to some kind of treatment or influence.

The people were to yield their will to God, by allowing the ark of the covenant to pass first, while they were to leave a space between them and the ark. Whenever God is leading, He always wants to have His way, not because He is all-powerful, but because He has been that way before, and He knows the end from the beginning.

Declaring the end from the beginning, and from ancient times the things that are not yet done, saying, My counsel shall stand, and I will do all my pleasure.
Isaiah 46:10

Our previous scripture (Psalm 127:1-2) says that unless the Lord builds the house, its builders labor over it in vain. It is not talking about a literal building; it is talking about your life. Except the Lord build your physical body and your spiritual life, you'll labor in vain trying to build it alone. Listen to me, you don't have to struggle doing this alone. Jesus is willing to build for you; all you need is to submit to His will.

Except the Lord watches over a city, the watchman stays alert in vain. Anything that is done or built without Jesus is in vain. It has no spiritual foundation as far as Jesus is concerned. He said, "I am the way, the truth, and the life: no man cometh to the Father, but by me" (John 14:6). So, if you're trying to get to God through some other means, Jesus said you're wasting your time; it's in vain. Stop trying to make that business succeed alone, stop trying to make that child obey alone, stop trying to make that marriage work alone, and stop trying to make that ministry grow alone. If you'll just put it in Master Jesus' hands, He will make a success out of it. Amen!

Jesus is a master builder, and He is saying, "Except I build your house, you'll labor in vain trying to build it. Except I keep your home, all who are trying to keep it are working in vain. What a shock! Could you imagine working all day long, and at the end of the day somebody tells you that everything you just did was in vain?

There was a well-built and well-fortified city called Jericho. The citizens of Jericho were not submitted to God; so they didn't commit their city to Him. Their trust was only in Jericho. They trusted the walls of that city, and they believed it wasn't possible ever, for anyone to invade and conquer their city. But to God, their strongholds were in vain. When God got ready, He said to Joshua His servant, "See, I have given Jericho into your hand, with its king and mighty men of valor." In the mind of God, the conquest of Jericho was a done deal; there was nothing to worry about.

He said to Joshua, "You shall march around the city, all the men of war shall go around it once. Thus shall you do for six days. Seven priests shall bear seven trumpets of rams' horns before the ark. On the seventh day you shall march around the city seven times, and the priests shall blow the trumpets, then all the people shall shout with a great shout, and the walls of that city will fall down flat, and the people shall go up every man straight before Him" (Joshua 6:3-5). That's how the walls of Jericho fell—by just a shout. The Israelites had spiritual powers working on their behalf. God was with them so that whatever they did prospered. Amen!

Another word I want us to look at is *build,* which means to **mold, form, create**, and **develop**. God is saying, "Except I form or shape you in my way, you will labor trying to do it yourself." Unless God shapes your thoughts to His thoughts, you will never understand His leading, and, therefore, you won't be able to fulfill His purpose in life. If you can't understand Him, then you won't be able to understand His mission, and you won't be able to fulfill His mission. That's why you must understand Him.

Seek ye the LORD while He may be found, call ye upon Him while He is near: Let the wicked forsake his way, and the unrighteous man his thoughts: and let him return unto the LORD, and He will have mercy upon him; and to our God, for He will abundantly pardon. For my thoughts are not your thoughts, neither are your ways my ways, saith the LORD. For as the heavens are higher than the earth, so are my ways higher than your ways and my thoughts than your thoughts.

Isaiah 55:6-9

If you allow God to shape your thoughts to His thoughts, then you'll be able to link your thoughts to His thoughts, and you'll be able to understand His mission as you follow Him. He said, as the heavens are higher than the earth, so are His thoughts higher than your thoughts, and His ways than your ways. This is why you must submit to Him. Amen.

Develop: to bring out the capabilities or possibilities of; bring to a more advanced or effective state; to cause to grow or expand, to cause to progress from an embryonic to an adult form.

God is saying, "Except I develop you and bring out your capabilities or possibilities, you'll labor in vine trying to do it yourself." Not all Christians are developed. Some are babes, and some are adults; some are still feeding on milk, and some are eating strong meat. Those who are still feeding on milk are the babes in Christ. They're the undeveloped Christians, and they always struggle to attend church services. They're still in the **accusing realm**. They are the ones who are always looking for the stakes in the eyes of their brothers and sisters. You know how little children behave. They say, "Dad, I want to be tall like you now! Why are you so tall and I am this short?" Not understanding that life is in stages, they don't know you have to grow up in order to arrive at the higher level. What a shock!

When I was a child, I spake as a child, I understood as a child, I thought as a child: but when I became a man, I put away childish things. For now we see through a glass, darkly; but then face to face: now I know in part; but then shall I know even as also I am known.
1 Corinthians 13:11-12

The apostle Paul said that when he was a child, he talked like a child and reasoned like a child; but when he became a man spiritually, he put the ways of childhood behind him. Then he said, "Now I know in part." Spiritual children can't know or understand in part. They have to develop and grow in order to know and understand in part. Jesus is willing to bring you to a more advanced or effective state, but you must be willing to follow Him and submit your will to His will. Then you will be able to grow in His will and understand what He is saying. Amen!

Let the Dead Bury Their Dead

And it came to pass, that, as they went in the way, a certain man said unto Him, Lord, I will follow thee whithersoever thou goest. And Jesus said unto him, Foxes have holes, and birds of the air have nests; but the Son of man hath not where to lay His head. And he said unto another, Follow me. But he said, Lord, suffer me first to go and bury my father. Jesus said unto him, Let the dead bury their dead: But go thou and preach the kingdom of God. And another also said, Lord, I will follow thee; but let me first go bid them farewell, which are at home at my house. And Jesus said unto him, No man, having put his hand to the plough, and looking back, is fit for the kingdom of God.
Luke 9:57-62

Another thing I want you to understand as you follow Jesus is your commitment to the service and calling of God upon your life. You must also understand the purpose of God for your life. Everyone who is born of God has the calling of God upon his or her life. The first purpose of God for every Christian is to preach the gospel of the kingdom of God to all nations till the end comes (Matthew 28:19-20). As you follow Jesus, He requires that from you every day of your life here on earth!

In the verses above, we see Jesus making a very strong and impressive statement. He told a certain man to follow Him, and the man replied, "Lord, first let me go and bury my father." Then Jesus said to him, "Let the dead bury their own dead, but you go and preach the kingdom of God." Now, what is Jesus really saying here? Is He saying He really doesn't care when we lose our loved ones or when somebody so dear to us is about to be taken away by death? No, No, No. Certainly you know and I know that physically dead people can't bury physically dead people. So, what is He saying then? Jesus is trying to make us understand that regardless of the situation we may be faced with today, we shouldn't allow that situation or problem to keep us from executing our assignment as soldiers of the Lord.

Even as you serve in a particular ministry, you may lose somebody very dear to you. Don't allow that situation—or anything that happens in your life—to keep you from preaching the gospel of God. If you allow that situation to distract you from preaching the gospel, it becomes a yoke from the devil. The sooner you understand this, the quicker you will be freed from that bondage. Let's read something the apostle Paul wrote to his son in the Lord, Timothy:

And if a man also strive for masteries, yet is he not crowned, except he strive lawfully. The husbandman that laboureth must be first partaker of the fruits. Consider what I say; and the Lord give thee understanding in all things. Remember that Jesus Christ of the seed of David was raised from the dead according to my gospel; wherein I suffer trouble, as an evil doer, even unto bonds; <u>but the word of God is not bound.</u> Therefore I endure all things for the elect's sakes that they may also obtain the salvation which is in Christ Jesus with eternal glory.
2 Timothy 2:5-10

The apostle Paul was telling Timothy what he had been through because of the gospel of Jesus. He was also encouraging him to be a good soldier of the Lord Jesus Christ. He said, "I suffer trouble as an evil doer, even unto bonds; but the **word of God is not bound**." I want you to understand this: you and I have a responsibility to Jesus Christ, and that is to never allow the Word of God to be bound. We must not allow circumstances to stop us from serving, worshiping, preaching, and doing what we have been called to do. Amen! Paul said even though he was in prison with chains, he would not be **quiet from preaching God's word**. I have never heard or seen a brother or sister in our day who has suffered like the apostle Paul did, and yet he still went on preaching the gospel of Jesus Christ.

You must understand that you're a soldier of the Lord Jesus Christ, and no soldier who is engaged in warfare and sees one of his fellow soldiers hit by a bullet will put his weapon down, turn around, and walk out of the battle. Instead, he will try to rescue his friend, while at the same time shooting at his enemies. You see, this is what Jesus meant when He said, "Let the dead bury their own dead": but you go and preach. From the day you decided to accept and follow Jesus as Lord and Savior of your life, you were enlisted in the army of Zion, and you were placed on the battlefield. So, Jesus is not saying you should not bury your dead or pay your last respects to them; He is saying you must not allow even the death of a loved one to stop you from following Him. And following Jesus is not just going to church on Sunday. It involves preaching, singing, evangelizing, praying, loving, etc.

Now a certain man was sick, name Lazarus, of Bethany, the town of Mary and her sister Martha. (It was that Mary which anointed the Lord with ointment, and wiped his feet with her hair, whose brother Lazarus was sick.) Therefore his sisters sent unto Him, saying, Lord, behold, he whom thou lovest is sick. When Jesus heard that, He said, This sickness is not unto death, but for the glory of God, that the Son of God might be glorified thereby.

Now Jesus loved Martha, and her sister, and Lazarus. When He had heard therefore that he was sick, He abode two days still in the same place where He was. Then after that saith He to His disciples, Let us go into Judaea again. His disciples say unto

Him, Master, the Jews of late sought to stone thee; and goest thou thither again? Jesus answered, Are there not twelve hours in the day? If any man walk in the day, he stumbleth not, because he seeth the light of this world.

But if a man walk in the night, he stumbleth, because there is no light in him. These things said He: and after that He saith unto them, Our friend Lazarus sleepeth; but I go, that I may awake him out of sleep. Then said His disciples, Lord if he sleep, he shall do well. Howbeit Jesus spake of his death: but they thought that he had spoken of taking of rest in sleep. Then said Jesus unto them plainly, Lazarus is dead. And I am glad for your sakes that I was not there, to the intent ye may believe; nevertheless let us go unto him. Then said Thomas, which is called Didymus, unto his fellow disciples, Let us also go, that we may die with Him.

John 11:1-16

This is a great story about Jesus' friend Lazarus. Jesus was somewhere beyond Jordan when He received the report that His friend Lazarus was sick, but He had already perceived that Lazarus was dead. Jesus was teaching when He received the news, but He didn't stop everything as soon He received that evil report. He continued to teach and preach. The Bible says that He stayed two more days in the same place. After that, Jesus told His disciples that Lazarus was dead, and then they went on the Bethany, where Lazarus was. Now, looking at this purely from the physical perspective, we might think Jesus was going to Bethany to pay His respects to His dead friend. But that is a faithless perspective. I want you to understand that Jesus was also willing to pay respect to the dead, but He would not forsake the purpose of His heavenly Father, which is to preach and teach the kingdom of God.

Since Jesus was a faith teacher, He refused always to acknowledge and say the negative. He was always in the positive when He walked this earth and is still in the positive today. He went to Bethany, not to accept that Lazarus was dead, but to raise him from the dead and announce the kingdom of God as He did before. Amen!

Forget Those Things behind You

In order to completely submit to Jesus, you must disconnect yourself from the past. You must forget the past, for you can't be fully submitted to Jesus until you stop meditating on those mistakes you have made. You must learn to forgive those people who hurt you years ago. You must learn to forget those painful moments from years back. You must learn to forget the sorrow, you must learn to forget that business you lost years ago, you must learn to forget that job you lost, you must learn to forget that marriage you lost, you must learn to forget that child you lost, and you must learn to forget that house you lost and that car you lost. Forget all those things, and move on with your life, because there is hope for your future in Jesus Christ. Amen!

Not as though I had already attained, either were already perfect: but I follow after, if that I may apprehend that for which also I am apprehended of Christ Jesus. Brethren, I count not myself to have apprehended: but this one thing I do, forgetting those things which are behind and reaching forth unto those things which are before, I press toward the mark for the prize of the high calling of God in Christ Jesus. Let us therefore, as many as be perfect, be thus minded: and if in anything ye be otherwise minded, God shall reveal even this unto you. Nevertheless, whereto we have already attained, let us walk by the same rule, let us mind the same thing.
Philippians 3:12-16

Paul the apostle is sharing with us something very powerful, something that can help us in our walk with Jesus. The apostle went through so many things because of the gospel of Jesus Christ. He was hurt by many evil religious people of his day, but he didn't give up preaching Christ Jesus everywhere he went. He said:

I have been in prison more frequently, been flogged more severely, and been exposed to death again and again. Five times I received from the Jews the forty lashes minus one. Three times I was beaten with rods, once I was pelted with stones, three times I was shipwrecked, I spent a night and a day in the open sea, and I have been constantly on the move. I have been in danger from rivers, in danger from bandits, in danger from my fellow Jews, in danger from Gentiles; in danger in the city, in danger in the country, in danger at sea; and in danger from false believers.

I have labored and toiled and have often gone without sleep; I have known hunger and thirst and have often gone without food; I have been cold and naked. Besides everything else, I face daily the pressure of my concern of all the churches. Who is weak, and I do not feel weak? Who is led into sin, and I do not inwardly burn? He said, if I must boast, I will boast of the things that show my weakness. In Damascus the governor under King Aretas had the city of the Damascenes guarded in order to arrest me. But I was lowered in a basket from a window in the wall and slipped through his hands

2 Corinthians 11:23-33 (NIV)

The apostle Paul went through many things during his missionary journeys, but still he said, "It is not as though I have arrived or am perfect. I count not myself to have understood everything; but this one thing I do: forgetting those things that are behind and reaching forth unto those things that are before, I press toward the mark for the prize of the high calling of God in Christ Jesus."

Now listen, he said the one thing he was doing was forgetting those things that were behind and reaching forth unto those things that were before. Why is it important to forget those things that are in the past? I believe one of reason is because they hold you back by holding your mind in the past. Every time you think on the past, you're moving one step behind, instead of moving forward. You don't want that. What you want is to keep moving forward and upward. That's the life of Jesus; that's the higher life. But this will only happen when you learn to forget the past and keep your focus on the future.

The apostle Paul did two things: (1) He forgot the past, and (2) he pressed toward the mark for the prize of the high calling of God in Christ Jesus. The high calling of God is in Jesus Christ, the Bible says, for it pleased the Father that in Him should all the **fullness**

dwell (Colossians 1:19). The Greek word for fullness is *pleroma*; so it pleased the Father that all the *pleroma* should dwell in Jesus. He is the foundation of the new covenant! This is one key for a successful life.

The Attitude of Lot's Wife

This is a story about Lot and his family. I want to show you why it's not a good attitude to keep focusing on the past rather than on the future.

And there came two angels to Sodom at even; and Lot sat in the gate of Sodom: and Lot seeing them rose up to meet them; and he bowed himself with his face toward the ground; And he said, Behold now, my lords, turn in, I pray you, into your servant's house, and tarry all night, and wash your feet, and ye shall rise up early, and go on your ways. And they said, Nay; but we will abide in the street all night. And he pressed upon them greatly; and they turned in unto him, and entered into his house; and he made them a feast, and did bake unleavened bread, and they did eat.

But before they lay down, the men of the city, even the men of Sodom, compassed the house round, both old and young, all the people from every quarter: And they called unto Lot, and said unto him, Where are the men which came in to thee this night? Bring them out unto us, that we may know them. And Lot went out at the door unto them, and shut the door after him, And said, I pray you, brethren, do not so wickedly. Behold now, I have two daughters which have not known man; let me, I pray you, bring them out unto you, and do ye to them as is good in your eyes: only unto these men do nothing; for therefore came they under the shadow of my roof.

And they said, Stand back. And they said again, this one fellow came in to sojourn, and he will needs be a judge: now will we deal worse with thee, than with them. And they pressed sore upon the man, even Lot, and came near to break the door. But the men put forth their hand, and pulled Lot into the house to them, and shut to the door. And they smote the men that were at the door of the house with blindness, both small and great: so that they wearied themselves to find the door.

And the men said unto Lot, Hast thou here any besides son in law, and thy sons, and thy daughters, and whatsoever thou hast in the city, bring them out of this place: For we will destroy this place, because the cry of them is waxen great before the face of the LORD; and the LORD hath sent us to destroy it. And Lot went out, and spake unto his sons in law, which married his daughters, and said, Up, get you out of this place; for the LORD will destroy this city. But he seemed as one that mocked unto his sons in law.

And when the morning arose, then the angels hastened Lot, saying, Arise, take thy wife, and thy two daughters, which are here; lest thou be consumed in the iniquity of the city. And while he lingered, the men laid hold upon his hand and upon the hand of his wife, and upon the hand of his two daughters; the LORD being merciful unto him: and they brought him forth, and set him without the city. And it came to pass, when they had brought them forth abroad, that he said, Escape for thy life; look not behind thee, neither stay thou in all the plain; escape to the mountain, lest thou be consumed. And Lot said unto them, Oh, not so, my Lord: Behold now, thy servant hath found grace in thy sight, and thou hast magnified thy mercy, which thou hast shewed unto me in saving my life; and I cannot escape to the mountain, lest some evil take me, and I die: Behold now, this city is near to flee unto, and it is a little one: Oh, let me escape thither, (is it not a little one?) and my soul shall live. And he said unto him, See, I have accepted thee concerning this thing also, that I will not overthrow this city, for the which thou hast spoken. Haste thee; escape thither; for I cannot do anything till thou become thither. Therefore the name of the city was called Zoar. The sun was risen upon the earth when Lot entered into Zoar.

Then the LORD rained upon Sodom and upon Gomorrah brimstone and fire from the LORD out of heaven; and he overthrew those cities and all the plain, and all the inhabitants of the cities, and that which grew upon the ground. <u>*But his wife looked back from behind him and she became a pillar of salt.*</u>

Genesis 19:1-26

Here is an interesting story about Abraham's nephew, Lot, and his family in Sodom. The sins of this nation had become a reproach in the sight of God, for the Bible says, righteousness exalts a nation, but sin is a reproach to any people (Proverbs 14:34). Because of this, God sent two angels to Sodom to destroy it and the city of Gomorrah. When they got there, it was a mess. The men of Sodom knew that Lot had received two strangers into his home. They went to the door, believing these strangers were men. They requested that the men be brought out so that they could have sex with them. What a shock!

This shows how sinful the men of Sodom and Gomorrah were, but in spite of all this, God still couldn't destroy the land because of the few righteous folks who were still living there; and because of His word, He can't destroy the wicked with the good. God had commanded the angels to destroy the land after Lot and his family had gone out of it. So, the next morning the angels said to Lot, "Hurry! Take your wife and your two daughters and leave now, for we can't do anything till you leave this place." When Lot lingered, the angels grasp him and his wife and their daughters by their hands and led them out of the city. Lot and his family really didn't want to leave that place, probably because they had invested a lot in the land. Probably, too, they were a bit confused about the fact that God was really going to destroy the land. All these things were in their minds; so they lingered.

When the angels brought them outside the city, one commanded them to not look back! You need to heed these words as well. Looking back will cost you your future and your life. It will keep you depressed for a very long time, it will slow down the process of achieving everything you desire to achieve in life, and it will keep your mind in bondage. That's why it's not a good thing to look back on the past. But Mrs. Lot decided to look back anyway, and she became a pillar of salt. She was too much into her past. She was too much into the things she had going on in Sodom and Gomorrah— that's what held her mind back. Be very careful as you walk with Jesus, not to keep your mind in the past. That's not a good attitude. A right attitude is when you keep your focus on Jesus continually. Amen!

Your Life Is in Him

For this commandment which I command thee this day, it is not hidden from thee, neither is it far off. It is not in heaven, that thou shouldest say, Who shall go up for us to heaven, and bring it unto us, that we may hear it, and do it? Neither is it beyond the sea, that thou shouldest say, Who shall go over the sea for us, and bring it unto us, that we may hear it, and do it? But the word is very nigh unto thee, in thy mouth, and in thy heart, that thou mayest do it.

See, I have set before thee this day life and good, and death and evil; In that I command thee this day to love the LORD thy God, to walk in his ways, and to keep his commandments and his statutes and his judgments, that thou mayest live and multiply: and the LORD thy God shall bless thee in the land whither thou goest to possess it. But if thine heart turn away, so that thou wilt not hear, but shalt be drawn away, and worship other gods, and serve them; I denounce unto you this day, that ye shall surely perish, and that ye shall not prolong your days upon the land, whither thou passest over Jordan to go to possess it.

I call heaven and earth to record this day against you, that I have set before you life and death, blessing and cursing: therefore choose life, that thou and thy seed may live: That thou mayest love the LORD thy God, and that thou mayest obey his voice, and that thou mayest <u>cleave unto him</u>: for he is thy life, and the length of thy days: that thou mayest dwell in the land which the LORD sware unto thy fathers, to Abraham, to Isaac, and to Jacob, to give them.

Deuteronomy 30:11-20

Moses, the servant of God, was reading out the commandment of God to the children of Israel as they prepared to go into and possess the land of Canaan that God promised their fathers. You must always be prepared to possess your possession, or you won't be able to maintain it after a while. Many of God's people pray for God to take them to a greater level in life, which is very good, but what do you do after you've been brought up to that level you've been praying and fasting for? Many quit praying and fasting as they did before, because of their enjoyment of the good life they're having in that new place. So I say, it's not enough to enter into your possession or to have new things; you also must be able to maintain whatever God has given to you!

For every higher level that you enter, there are **higher demons** ready to tempt you and to cause the attention of evil people to be drawn toward you. If you're going to maintain your possession, you must always be prepared and ready in prayer and studying God's Word. So Moses was getting them ready by reading out to them the commandments of God and showing them the mind of God concerning them as they entered into that new place.

He was actually saying, "God has set before you today life and prosperity, death and destruction; but you're commanded today to love the Lord your God, walk in obedience to him, and keep His commands, decrees, and laws. This day I have set before you life and death, blessings and curses. Choose life, so that you and your children may live and that you may love the Lord your God, listen to his voice, and hold fast to him, for the Lord is your life and the length of your days." So, in other words, he was saying, "Your life is in God. That's why you must hold Him fast, that's why you must follow Him wherever He is going or leading you."

Jesus said, "If anyone is thirsty, let him come to me and drink" (John 7:37 NIV). If you're thirsty for the Holy Spirit, Jesus is calling you today to come to Him. He is your life and the length of your days. He will give you rest.

Come unto me, all ye that labour and are heavy laden and I will give you rest. Take my yoke upon you, and learn of me; for I am meek and lowly in heart: and ye shall find rest unto your souls. For my yoke is easy, and my burden is light.
Matthew 11:28-30

Jesus was talking here about rest for your soul and spirit, not rest from this life or work. As long as you're in this world, you'll still have to work; but you don't have to be in fear all your life. You don't have to be depressed because of the troubles in this world. If you follow Jesus, He is able to keep you from the fears of life and keep you in His peace. There is the peace of Jesus, and there is the peace of this world. The peace of Jesus never fails; it's always fresh and new and is able to keep you from the evil of this world—but it is available to you only if you'll have faith in Jesus and follow Him!

And one of the company said unto Him, Master, speak to my brother, that he divide the inheritance with me. And He said unto him, Man, who made me a Judge or a divider over you? And He said unto them, Take heed, and beware of covetousness: for a man's life consisteth not in the abundance of the things which he possesseth. And he spake a parable unto them, saying, The ground of a certain rich man brought forth plentifully: And he thought within himself, saying, What shall I do, because I have no room where to bestow my fruits? And he said, This will I do: I will pull down my barns, and build greater; and there will I bestow all my fruits and my goods. And I will say to my soul, Soul, thou hast much goods laid up for many years; take thine ease, eat, drink, and be merry. But God said unto him, Thou fool, this night thy soul shall be required of thee: then whose shall those things be, which thou hast provided? So is he that layeth up treasure for himself, <u>and is not rich toward God</u>.

Luke 12:13-21

As I said previously, your life is in Jesus. I will continue to say this because I want it to create an image in your mind that will help you follow Jesus. Here He was speaking a parable, telling us why we must not trust in people or things, for our lives don't consist in the abundance of the things we have. Your life is not in your job, and neither is it in your career or your children. Many people—even many Christians—have not come to understand this truth yet. That's why many are willing to go the extra mile for their company, career, job, children, relationships, and businesses but not for the work of God. And they will always have excuses. Often, they will say their safety comes first. That's wrong. What comes first is not your safety, it's not your family's safety, and it's not your job's safety. What comes first is **Jesus and His kingdom.**

Jesus Himself said that whoever tries to keep his life will lose it, and whoever loses his life will preserve it (Luke 17:33). We are seeing this happen today. Many who have the best security in this world are the ones being affected by the evil of this world, while the simple, or the babes of the kingdom of God, are being saved in the midst of death and the evil of this world. Brothers and sisters, don't be deceived. Jesus is able to save you and keep you in divine peace (John 14:27). Trust Jesus, and follow Him with your whole heart, and your life will never be the same. Amen!

Prayer of Salvation

I want you to know that Jesus' love for you is greater than any other person you know today. He came and laid down His life and rose again just for you and me, so that we could spend eternity with Him in heaven and experience His peace, joy, and blessings here on earth. If you would like to receive Jesus Christ into your life today, say the following prayer out loud right now, and mean it from your heart!

Heavenly Father, I come to you, admitting that I am a sinner. Right now, I choose to turn away from sin, and I ask you to cleanse me of all unrighteousness. I believe that your son, Jesus, died on the cross to take away my sins. I also believe that He rose again from the dead so that I might be forgiven of my sins and made righteous through faith in Him. I call upon the name of Jesus Christ to be the Savior and Lord of my life. Jesus, I choose to follow You, and I ask that you fill me with the power of the Holy Spirit. I declare that right now I am a child of God. I am free from sin, and I am full of the righteousness of God. I am saved right now in Jesus' Name. Amen!

Jesus Himself said that whoever tries to keep his life will lose it, and whoever loses his life will preserve it (Luke 17:33). We are seeing this happen today. Many who have the best security in this world are the ones being affected by the evil of this world, while the simple, or the babes of the kingdom of God, are being saved in the midst of death and the evil of this world. Brothers and sisters, don't be deceived. Jesus is able to save you and keep you in divine peace (John 14:27). Trust Jesus, and follow Him with your whole heart, and your life will never be the same. Amen!

Prayer of Salvation

I want you to know that Jesus' love for you is greater than any other person you know today. He came and laid down His life and rose again just for you and me, so that we could spend eternity with Him in heaven and experience His peace, joy, and blessings here on earth. If you would like to receive Jesus Christ into your life today, say the following prayer out loud right now, and mean it from your heart!

Heavenly Father, I come to you, admitting that I am a sinner. Right now, I choose to turn away from sin, and I ask you to cleanse me of all unrighteousness. I believe that your son, Jesus, died on the cross to take away my sins. I also believe that He rose again from the dead so that I might be forgiven of my sins and made righteous through faith in Him. I call upon the name of Jesus Christ to be the Savior and Lord of my life. Jesus, I choose to follow You, and I ask that you fill me with the power of the Holy Spirit. I declare that right now I am a child of God. I am free from sin, and I am full of the righteousness of God. I am saved right now in Jesus' Name. Amen!

www.ingramcontent.com/pod-product-compliance
Ingram Content Group UK Ltd.
Pitfield, Milton Keynes, MK11 3LW, UK
UKHW022222230426
12048UKWH00016BA/1015